GOD Used a Cigarette

GOD Used a Cigarette

Craig Sneddon

with Virginia Sneddon

Tate Publishing & *Enterprises*

GOD Used a Cigarette

Published by Tate Publishing & Enterprises, LLC
127 E. Trade Center Terrace | Mustang, Oklahoma 73064 USA
1.888.361.9473 | www.tatepublishing.com

Tate Publishing is committed to excellence in the publishing industry. The company reflects the philosophy established by the founders, based on Psalm 68:11,
"The Lord gave the word and great was the company of those who published it."

Cover design by April Marcizewski
Interior design by Chelsea Womble

Published in the United States of America

ISBN: 978-1-61777-524-6
1. Religion, Christian Life, Relationships
2. Biography & Autobiography, Personal Memoirs
11.05.13

To Kenny and Trish. We love y'all!

Acknowledgements

Craig would like to thank the following people for making this book possible:

Maw, for never giving up on me all those years where it seemed I was on a one-way train to total destruction and for always being the kindest and most understanding mother I could never deserve.

Graeme, for saving my life on so many occasions. You are a gentleman and a confidante to so many people, and it is an honor to have you as my best friend.

The Gran, for your constant prayers, the wee notes, and all the gifts. You are the best!

Vickie, for your hugs, your songs, and all the things you write to me. You truly light up my life, and it's hard having you live so far away.

Mark, for being so unique and for giving me a reason to come back to San Antonio that second time. Keep believing!

Alan and Cathie, for being such dear friends and for stepping in and being available on so many occasions.

And for my beautiful wife, Gina, for all the reasons contained in this book and for making the days and months since our marriage the best of my life. I love you all so much more than a few lines could ever say.

Virginia would like to thank the following people for their love and support:

Dad, Mom, Carol, and John, who all helped shape me into the person I am today.

Eartha, my friend, companion, and sister in Christ who always has a timely word and whose fruit is genuine like her passion for the Lord.

Alma, a constant source of prayer and biblical encouragement.

Samuel and Babette, and Kevin and Lisa, for all your love and advice and for being such a strong support in my life.

Michael and Ryna, for supplying a steady flow of scripture and demonstrating the love of Jesus as my cell group leaders.

Pastor John Hagee, for being a spiritual father to me during every stage of my adult life.

The Cornerstone Music Department, for allowing me to serve my God in song.

Craig and Virginia would jointly like to thank the following people: Our wonderful children: Cassandra, Joseph, and Jacob for embracing this new family of ours and for making us proud in all you do each and every day.

Pastor John and Diana Hagee and Pastor Matthew Hagee for all your spiritual guidance and teaching. It is truly an unparalleled blessing to be under your authority.

And of course, our Lord and Savior, Jesus Christ, without Whom our union would never have taken place. Life without Your love would not be worth living.

Unless the Lord builds the house, they labor in vain who build it...

Psalm 127:1

Introduction

The Bible tells us to "seek first the kingdom of God and His righteousness" (Matthew 6:33). God "is a rewarder of those who diligently seek Him" (Hebrews 11:6).

In *God Used a Cigarette*, these two verses go hand in hand. Hidden in its exciting storyline are lessons of faith from many different angles not limited to those either in or seeking a relationship.

May this story bless and encourage those who have an existing belief in Christ Jesus as well as those who are not yet there; it has been written with both in mind.

God is indeed good!

Chapter One

Jim walked to the edge of the church parking lot, stood by the road, and lit up a cigarette. He'd just come out of the most amazing church service he'd ever been to in which he promised himself and God that he was ready for a fresh start and an escape from past vices; yet here he was still desperate for nicotine to satisfy the two-hour gap since the last one.

Ah well, he thought. The first couple of inhalations felt good. So good, in fact, that when seconds later a cab came into view, he decided to let it pass in favor of the cigarette. He believed that since one cab came along within a minute, then there should be another one not far behind it. Twenty minutes and one more cigarette later, there were no more cabs to be seen, and he began to wonder what to do next. Originally, to get to the church, he'd taken the bus from his hotel, but it had only gone part of the way there, and he'd ended up walking four miles from where it had dropped him off. Walking the four miles back to the bus stop and hoping there were still buses operating at that time of night was not feasible because it was dark, he was tired, and he didn't have enough cigarettes to last the duration and the stores were now closed.

Jim was in San Antonio on an escape from the realities of life back in the UK. His father had recently passed away after a long battle with cancer and a brain tumor, he had to sell his home and leave his friends to move south to settle some debts and be closer to his remaining family, and he'd recently returned to work after a long absence due to alcoholism and depression. Two months into his new life, he'd already had enough of things and was in need of some cheering up.

So it was that one day, while watching Christian television, he saw an advertisement for a "celebration weekend" at a large church in San Antonio, Texas. The three-day event was to include fairground rides and fireworks, lots of food, live music, and dancing, but, above all, he would see two of his favorite TV preachers sharing the one platform, which to him seemed too good to miss. He only had to see the advertisement once, but with eight hundred pounds that his mother had given him as a share of his father's estate, he thought, *Why not?*

Having attended the first night—the Friday night—he felt physically tired but spiritually invigorated, waiting by the side of the road in the dark for a cab. Eventually he decided to see if he could find someone who could help him, and he walked back to the main entrance. As he got to the door, a man was coming out of the building.

"Excuse me," Jim said. "Can you tell me where I can phone for a taxi please?" His strong Scottish accent let the man know right away he wasn't a native of Texas.

"Where are you going?" the man asked, to which Jim pulled out his map and pointed to where his hotel was situated.

"Well, we can take you there. Come on. Come with us," said the man, and he led Jim to his car. "I'm Steve by the way," he said, offering out his hand for Jim to shake. "And my wife's name is Diane." Diane was already waiting in the car.

"I'm Jim. Nice to meet you!" Jim replied, inwardly thanking God for the free ride.

Steve was an ex-serviceman, just past retirement age, although he still looked young and was still full of youthful energy. He had a wacky sense of humor and an adventurous streak—similar to Jim's own—as well as a big heart. Diane was a few years younger than he was, and her more sedate nature balanced well against his zany personality, bringing him into check whenever he got too carried away, as he often did.

"What y'all doing in Texas?" he asked Jim once they'd exited the church parking lot.

"Oh, I'm just here on holiday—sorry, vacation—and to attend the celebration weekend that you're having," said Jim, trying his best to substitute his UK dialect for American whenever he could remember.

"Y'all are just here to go to church?" Diane asked.

"Aye, just me myself." Jim answered, indirectly addressing the "y'all" part of Diane's question, unaware that it was a term used a lot in Texas even when addressing a single person. Steve later joked that if addressing more than one person it then became "all y'all!"

In truth, Jim was a committed Christian who loved God dearly and had since he gave his heart to him at the age of three. Yet for a long time, he had led a sinful life, choosing sex and alcohol over righteous living. At this point in his life, age thirty-three, he had journeyed far down his road to recovery but still had a good deal further to go; there were still many things in his life that needed attention, but the revelation that God had saved him from an early grave left him regularly thankful. And now, following the commitment he'd just made about an hour earlier in the church service to forsake the things that habitually held him back, he was determined that this was to be the beginning of better things to come.

Around fifteen minutes later, they reached the hotel where Jim was staying. Steve gave him his cell phone number and offered to pick him up the following afternoon and drive over to the church to enjoy the festivities that were taking place all afternoon. He had earlier resigned himself to being unable to attend the Saturday evening service owing to the difficulties he had in getting there on the Friday, so this offer of a ride was just fantastic, and he readily accepted. He thanked them both and subsequently spent a good deal of time in his hotel room thanking God.

The following morning he spent a few hours touring downtown San Antonio by himself before returning to his hotel where he was picked up as promised by Steve and Diane. They took him to the church and introduced them to a number of their friends, all of whom had the same reaction as Diane had the night before: "Y'all came all this way just to go to church?"

The food, the rides, the hot October sunshine, and the welcoming company of those to whom he was introduced all felt great, and Jim was enjoying every moment of it. He couldn't wait to get on the phone to his family to let them know just how good it was here! He pondered for a moment whether he would like to live in San Antonio but dismissed it as fantasy and didn't give it any further thought.

The Saturday evening came, and there was another service held that night, this time with a different guest speaker from the night before. Steve and Diane were well-connected within the church, so they were able to obtain three seats right in the center and near the front of the six-thousand-seat auditorium. *This weekend just keeps getting better and better!* Jim thought to himself.

The service began, and as the musicians commenced playing, two enormous curtains which divided the back of the stage from the front were pulled to each side and exposed a robed choir of around one hundred and fifty members who began singing with fervor. Jim smiled as a warm shiver ran down his spine. He hadn't been to anything like this before. He hadn't experienced it the previous night, either, since he had arrived late. He joined in with an energy and a volume unlike anything he'd ever done before as he worshipped with the rest of the huge congregation, singing the old choruses. He pictured heaven as being something similar and felt like he just couldn't get enough!

The huge choir took over and performed two high-tempo songs that had the whole congregation on their feet in appreciation, not only for the talent on display, but also for the Lord in Whom they greatly rejoiced. The noise was incredible! Jim was enraptured by the whole experience, but at the same time he was drawn to one particular singer in the center of the front row, almost directly in front of where he was standing. She had a radiant smile, which seemed to be a permanent feature the whole time she was on stage. She worshipped with zest and energy, and all her heart and soul was poured into her singing. Soon his gaze was fixated solely upon her. The rest of the choir seemed to fade into the background. And while he watched her he thought, *If only I could know what it is to worship like she does.*

He tried to pry his eyes away from her. Church was not the place to be studying the opposite sex, yet since he was admiring her worship, he found his actions justified. Physically, yes, she was attractive, but on this occasion, it was not as important to him as any other time he'd observed someone he liked in the past. All he could focus on in this instance was her energy and her obvious love of the Lord.

His mind started to wander. He thought if he were to bump into her after the service, he would tell her what an encouragement she was to him and how inspired he was by her. That's all—that's all he would say to her just to encourage her in return. He knew he was only on a four-day vacation and never likely to return, so doing anything else like asking her out on a date would be a futile thing to do. But just to get the chance to talk with her for a moment and to see her smile up close would satisfy his curiosity.

The curtain closed after the choir's performance, and the powerful preaching that followed stole his mind away from the woman he'd been watching. Even though he ultimately didn't get to meet her, it had still been a wonderful night, and he went back to his hotel buzzing with energy. There would be a regular service the following morning at the church and another special event the following night, and he couldn't wait to attend both of them.

The morning service followed a similar pattern as the night before, and once the congregational praise and worship had finished, the choir came forward with another two songs. There she was again in the same spot in the front row, shining brightly and giving it her all. The same thoughts as the night before flooded Jim's mind as he pondered what he would say to her if the six thousand to one chance of bumping into her actually took place.

The special event at the church consisted of various guest speakers and musical performances as well as a drama presentation in which Steve and Diane were involved. Since they needed to be there early for a final rehearsal, Jim went with them and was allowed backstage, where he watched them prepare. At the start of the proceedings, however, due to a late call-off, there were insufficient people to help with the preparations for one particular scene, so Jim was called to lend a hand. Later, another cast member dropped out at the last minute, and Jim was asked if he could play the part instead. It was a non-speaking part and didn't involve much acting, but it involved being dressed in costume and carrying a large banner through the auditorium and onto the stage. Feeling honored, he readily accepted both requests with excitement and donned his costume.

While waiting for his next instruction, he stood near a door with his back against the wall. The fact that the event was to be televised worldwide on Christian television and the fear of making a mistake was causing his heart to beat slightly faster. He turned his neck and head in a full circle to rid himself of some tension. As he neared the end of his second rotation, he spotted the woman he'd been admiring standing not more than five feet away from him.

Jim was never afraid to speak to anyone. His amiable personality won him many friends, and his outgoing nature was never offensive. He certainly didn't have a problem approaching women. He turned to speak to the woman next to him, opened his mouth to speak, and said ...nothing! Nothing came out!

He tried again: mouth open, tongue moving, yet still no words were coming out! He tried a third time, then a fourth: still nothing! One consolation was that she was facing forward and didn't see his muted attempts to engage her. But this was certainly strange. How could he be talking yet nothing was happening? All he wanted to say was, "Hey, the way you worship the Lord is inspiring to me," and then see her reaction, see if she'd smile.

"Hi, it's Jim isn't it? Come this way." Another member of the drama cast led him away. A quick glance back let him know that she hadn't seen him at all, and she was still facing in the same direction. All he could think of was it was the nerves of walking out in front of so many people that had gotten the better of him and had caused him to fail so miserably. He turned his attention back to the task at hand—his part in the drama—but couldn't help replaying the incident in his mind a number of times before he went into the auditorium. *It was just the weirdest thing!*

His performance in the drama and the rest of the evening both went well, and he left feeling proud to have been a part of it all. It took a long while and quite a few cigarettes in his hotel room that night before he was able to get to sleep. The main thing keeping him awake, however, was not his part in the proceedings but rather his inability to say just a couple of things to someone he probably wasn't going to see again in his life. *Just what exactly happened there?*

The next morning Steve and Diane came by the hotel early with some DVDs containing the recordings of the weekend's services. Steve now worked part-time in the church's TV studios assisting them with their DVD packaging, and, as a result, he was able to obtain early copies of all the services that took place at the church.

Jim thanked him for his trouble. He and Steve had become close over the course of the weekend. While he was sad to be leaving, he could now look forward to showing his family back home just how awesome the services were and also to secretly see whether the DVDs showed any of the girl with the nice smile singing.

The three exchanged embraces and prayed in the parking lot for a safe journey back to the UK. He later took a cab to the airport, and as his plane took off, he gazed out of the window and bid farewell to San Antonio. While Diane had told him he was welcome to come back and stay with them any time, it didn't seem like that was likely to happen.

Chapter Two

Five months later, Jim was back in San Antonio.

This time his brother Martin was with him and they had taken up Steve and Diane's offer for them to stay at their house. Martin was originally supposed to accompany him on his first trip, but a problem with his passport meant he was refused travel when he arrived at the airport. Jim felt bad for him at the time and had paid an extra seventy-five dollars for his ticket to be kept open for a year.

It had been hard for Jim to contain his excitement in front of Martin after he had returned home the first time. In one sense he wanted to emphasize what a fantastic time he'd had, yet he knew that Martin was absolutely devastated about not making it, and so he tried hard to play it down. Martin was two years older than he, but had a condition that meant his mental age was somewhat younger and, therefore, made his disappointment greater. He was perfectly competent in most areas of his life but required extra supervision and assistance in others.

Now here they were in Texas together after a successful second attempt. Jim had unleashed his previously-restrained excitement on Martin on the plane journey over, recounting the stories he had withheld from him the first time, and now Martin was beginning to understand why he was so happy to be back. He was having a great time too! The hospitality and generosity of Steve and Diane was second to none, and for the best part of eleven days, they showed them a whole lot of what Texas had to offer.

Near the end of their stay, while resting in the house in the evening, Steve put on a DVD of another event that had been held at the church. They were able to watch the choir perform some more songs, and as the camera focused on the woman who had captivated Jim so much the first time he visited San Antonio, he finally asked Steve, "Who is that woman?"

"Which woman?" Steve asked.

"The one in the front row with all the enthusiasm who just never seems to stop smiling! She's got the most amazing smile! And the way she worships . . . I mean . . . I just wish I could catch some of what she's got! She's incredible!"

"Yeah, she is somethin'! I think her name's Maria," Diane said, totally unaware of the full extent of the feelings for Maria that Jim was harboring inside. Just learning her name brought about an inward satisfaction, as if he were already getting closer!

"Want me to hook you guys up?" Steve asked with a wry smile.

"Aye, I guess you could!" Jim said with fake sincerity. He never for a minute thought Steve was serious, so he played along.

"Don't be silly!" said Martin. "I mean, what are you going to do if she says yes? You can't exactly go out with her when she's over here, and you're over there."

"It *could* work!" said Jim, rebuking Martin for pouring scorn on his private little fantasy! Martin had a quizzical way of thinking in any given situation, but once he had established his own logic to it, in his mind there was nothing that could be done to shift it. No amount of persuasive explaining or intelligent reasoning. And this was something that, despite being Martin's brother all these years, always seemed to irritate Jim and provoke the wrong response in him. It was best to let him alone to his juvenile thoughts and opinions and just let him be content in them, but for some reason

Jim always felt the need to set the record straight even though it did little good.

"Sure it could!" Steve said.

"Oh, Honey, don't be silly!" Diane said with a smile. "How do you know she's not married anyway?"

"I don't think she is," Jim answered, now steering his fantasy into the realms of reality. "I've already checked her wedding finger, and I couldn't see any ring there."

"Well, I'll ask her for you," Steve said.

"Cool!" said Jim, with sarcastic joy. But then with an exaggerated tone of disappointment he said, "Actually, we gotta go home in a couple of day's time so it wouldn't be worth it. Thanks anyway!"

"You could stay on a bit," Steve continued, not wanting the frivolities to end. "It's our pastor's fiftieth anniversary of ministry next weekend, and they're having a big event at the church's country retreat. I imagine she'll be going to that. You could ask her out yourself then."

This lit a fuse inside of Jim! He actually *could* go to the event because he still had the whole of the next eight days off work. The only reason they were going home on the Monday was because he felt that eleven days were long enough to take advantage of Steve and Diane's hospitality; plus he reckoned it was about as long as his patience levels would hold out having to look after Martin the whole time. In addition, Martin had his disability benefit to collect once he got back, so he *had* to return. Undeterred by this, Jim's mind started racing. He jumped up hurriedly and asked if he could use Steve's computer. He figured if the price were low enough, he could escort Martin back to the UK then return a day or two later for the weekend. He didn't care about jetlag or it affecting his eventual return to work. He wasn't even dwelling on Maria that much at this point either. He just wanted to be back in Texas and enjoy more time with his hosts by himself, and the anniversary party seemed too good to miss!

A search engine revealed available flights at a very low price. He would return to San Antonio on the Thursday and leave again on the Sunday afternoon, getting him home on the Monday before starting work the following day. "Champion!" Jim shouted and proceeded to book them.

The weekend passed, and he and Martin returned to the UK, arriving back in London on the Tuesday morning. The next day Jim was admitted to hospital. Although he hadn't told anyone, the whole time he had been in San Antonio he had been experiencing severe chest and back pains together with shortness of breath and pain in one of his legs and feet. Aside from having to escort Martin home, it was another reason why he didn't simply remain in San Antonio for the whole week, opting to make use of the UK medical system, which wouldn't cost him any money. He spent a lot of the return journey home begging God to allow him to make it safely back without it turning into an incident on the plane. God obliged, so he went to the hospital.

A chest x-ray and other factors seemed to indicate blood clots on his lungs, and further tests would be required to establish the exact nature of his condition. This involved being kept in overnight with the likelihood of a further eight days in hospital if the doctor's original fears were realized. One thing was certain: he wasn't going back to San Antonio the next day.

He called his mother to let her know. When she eventually composed herself after hearing the news, she made some calls to her Christian friends to ask them to pray and then to Steve and Diane to inform them that Jim would not be coming. She was also able to obtain a refund of most of the airfare he had paid out for his trip back to San Antonio, but this was little consolation to Jim who was more upset at not being able to return to Texas than hearing of his potentially life-threatening condition. Lying in his hospital bed that evening, he briefly thought of Maria and came to the conclusion that since this was the second time he'd been unable to meet her that God really didn't want him to.

He woke up the next morning feeling surprisingly good. The pain that had dogged his body for the last few weeks was notably absent, and all that was left was extreme fatigue, which at least still made him *look* ill! He underwent a full-body scan and gave blood samples, and the nurses continued to monitor his temperature and blood pressure at regular intervals.

Early that same afternoon, the doctor came round with the news. "It isn't anything like what we first thought," he said. "We're still not exactly sure what it is, but we should know from the blood test results. You're free to go home just now, though. Make an appointment for next week at the outpatients' clinic, and we'll take it from there."

Jim did as instructed, and the following week, he was back in the hospital for his appointment. After a three-hour wait, he was finally told that his blood test results had not yet come back, to return home, and to call his own doctor the next day as they would be arranged to be sent there. That following day he was informed that his blood samples had gone missing! Determined to get to the bottom of his illness, he made an appointment to give more blood samples at a separate clinic five days later. He attended the clinic but forgot his documentation and was turned away again. A week later he finally provided more samples. At the end of nearly four weeks, he was given the same news he'd received in the hospital: "We're not exactly sure what it was, but whatever was there isn't there now. You're all clear."

To Jim, this news was still an irritation. He'd been scared by a seemingly incorrect diagnosis of a very serious condition; he'd used up some of his time off work attending hospital, and, above all, he'd missed out on a once-in-a-lifetime anniversary celebration in his new favorite place to be.

To everyone else, God had healed him.

A month later he was back in hospital for a pre-arranged operation on a hernia. The night before the operation, the plane on which he was working in his capacity as a flight attendant was struck by lightning shortly after take-off. No one was hurt, and the plane made a safe landing, but an inspection revealed that it could have been catastrophic had the lightning struck just one inch further up from where it did. When he returned home late that evening, he was sure he heard God say to him, "I'm still in control."

In the recovery time that followed his operation and fuelled by yet another near-death experience on the airplane, he reflected on where he was in life and found that he didn't like what he was discovering. He hated that he was living in a tiny single-room apartment (which he nicknamed "The Shoebox"), he hated his job, he hated the fact he was unable to drive due to a lengthy ban imposed on him for drunk-driving, he hated his "alcoholic" label, and he especially bemoaned the fact that he was still single. And now, unable to move very far because of the pain and the stitches in his wound, he repeatedly took out his frustrations on God. *I've tithed! I've made proclamations! I've prayed! I've read Your Word! I've cleaned up my act*! he thought, yet at the end of each rant, he always simply heard God say, "I'm still in control." Despite knowing better, being aware of all the previous times God had come through for him and spending a great deal of his recovery time watching Christian TV, it still seemed difficult to believe.

At least he had one thing to look forward to in all his misery: four weeks' sick leave was immediately followed by twelve days' vacation time for which he'd purposefully arranged and booked another trip to the United States. This time he would take in four different cities, the last one again being San Antonio where he'd spend a few days with Steve and Diane.

He began his trip in Washington DC where he spent just a couple of days sightseeing. From there he flew to Columbus, Ohio. The only reason he wanted to go to Columbus was to attend the church of the guest preacher he'd heard in San Antonio the previous year at the celebration event. Since being so impressed by him, he had gotten further resources and had become a regular contributor to his ministry. And despite his faltering faith, he still desired to seek God, and this seemed like a good way to kick-start it again.

The morning service at the church was excellent even though the pastor's regular preaching sermon was replaced by various tributes to the armed forces on account that it was Memorial Day weekend in America. In the evening service, his preaching spot was filled by his mother who, in her own fiery style, demonstrated the hereditary family zeal—she was loud yet inspiring, and Jim was not disappointed. Her message focused on the concept of "give, and it will be given to you," as taught by Jesus, using the agricultural aspect of sowing and reaping to illustrate her point (Luke 6:38). At the end she encouraged the congregation to demonstrate their faith in God's word by sowing a financial seed and writing on their respective contribution envelopes their greatest desire in life that they would like to see God provide as harvest in response to their giving. On Jim's envelope he wrote, "WIFE." The man next to him wrote "TRUCK" on his, and he couldn't help thinking that the man's request was a whole lot easier for God to handle!

From Columbus, a couple of days later, he flew to New Orleans where he would spend two nights. On the first night, he ate dinner at a restaurant before retiring to his hotel early. The following day he discovered New Orleans' hedonistic reputation as he wandered the French Quarter and the infamous Bourbon Street.

Bourbon Street was filled with restaurants, clubs, and bars and notable strip joints. Only two years earlier, Jim would have fallen love with such a street, and, had he known that this particular place existed at the time, it would've been a safe bet that he'd have gone there with the intention of drinking himself into oblivion. From the age of fifteen, he'd quickly discovered the pull of alcohol, and it was something that would dominate his life and weaken his faith in God for the next sixteen years, almost to the brink of death; such was the extent of his addiction. It began with the need for a "good time"—partying and hanging out with so-called friends—but became a point of refuge during lonely times, of which there became many as all the friends he clung to so often let him down. The girlfriends came and went, his best friend of ten years robbed and betrayed him, and his father embarked on two affairs, all of which had a profound effect on his overly-trusting nature. Violence and pornography later occupied the shelves where his Bible once stood. And the need for Jesus was replaced by a crushing need for alcohol as he became critically dependent to the point where he was unable to leave his house except under the control of a quart of whisky. Only God kept him alive until he was ready to face facts and get help, as, to the rest of the world, he was dead for sure. And only with God's help did he ultimately overcome his addiction.

Now, here in New Orleans, he was reminded of his past. The girls, the bars, the smell of smoke, and the loud music was everywhere. Yet instead of fleeing from it, he was experiencing a strong urge to participate. A doorman handed him a coupon entitling him to free entry to Bourbon Street's only fully-nude strip club and did his best to persuade him to come in. "Later!" Jim said, with an unwelcome feeling that he might actually take him up on it. And a desire for alcohol overtook him unlike any other he'd felt since he first quit drinking two years ago.

Eventually he forced himself back to his hotel where he reflected on how close he'd come to submitting to a night of debauchery, smoking about ten cigarettes in succession to relieve his tension. *What happened there?* Only the knowledge of having to board a plane and visiting Steve and Diane the following day kept him from having a drink. Were he going elsewhere, he definitely would have succumbed, that's for certain, and the chances are he would not have left New Orleans either. At one point during the planning stage of his vacation, he'd almost decided not to include San Antonio in his travel plans; as a result of his escape from New Orleans, he was now glad he did. The fact that he'd never be able to tell Steve and Diane that he'd been in America without coming to visit them won over his decision to go there in the end. And shortly after being picked up at the airport he was glad he did.

"I've got you a date!" said Steve with pride!

Chapter Three

Jim had come to realize that there was nothing Steve was afraid to do. All too often when they were out together, Steve would crack jokes or start conversations with complete strangers and say some of the most outlandish things, all in the name of fun! So he knew that he was not afraid of approaching anyone and that this date thing was probably true. Instead of getting excited, though, his heart immediately sank at the thought of having to entertain some potentially ugly spinster whom Steve had picked out at random.

"Oh yeah?" Jim asked warily.

"Actually I've got you two dates—one for Saturday night and one for Sunday afternoon."

This was even worse!

"Who with?"

"Remember, I introduced you to a girl the first time you were here? Her name's Violet. She has black hair, and she's about your age. She was in the same drama you were in at the festival."

"Yeah," Jim said, his fears being somewhat realized. Violet at least was far from ugly, but she wasn't his type, and for a moment he even became slightly angry. "Who's the other one?" he asked, trying to divert the conversation away from his disappointment.

"Remember that girl you liked in the choir—Maria?"

"The one with the nice smile?" Jim asked, his joy instantly restored.

"Uh huh. We're going out to lunch with her after she's finished singing at second service."

"What did you say to her?" Jim asked, his joy suddenly turning to fear as he thought about how Steve might have already embarrassed him in his approaching of her.

"Just…somethin'!"

"What, exactly?"

"Just…somethin'! I just told her you liked her."

That was all Jim was going to get out of him. He turned to look out the window, his heart racing, as he immediately contemplated his opening line to Maria as well as how he was going to keep his date with her out of the conversation when he met with Violet, and how he was going to have to let her down gently. As it turned out, Violet unexpectedly had to go out of town the next day, and the date was cancelled, leaving Jim able to concentrate all his thoughts on his lunch with Maria.

In the next two days that followed, Jim was unable to think of anything other than meeting Maria. Going on a blind date was not a new experience to him, and this was not what was keeping him awake at night. So many things kept entering his mind.

Jim had prayed that the next woman he dated would be the one he married. He'd grown tired of starting relationships only to see them end again and, therefore, prayed a prerequisite over his next one. He would later realize that his request was linked to his long period of remaining single—God was answering his prayer!

Considering his prayer, he resolved not to view Sunday's lunch with Maria as a date. After all, how could he possibly marry someone from America? *That's just crazy man thinking! No! There's no way she'd be up for it either! She's probably just humoring Steve anyway! God, there must be some mistake! You remember what I prayed too, right? Don't You think that's a bit cruel? How can I possibly date some-*

one who's five thousand miles away anyway? Plus I'm going home on Monday. I'd only see her once! What could possibly come out of one meeting? This is insane...And so it went on inside his head.

The second thing that occupied his mind was something that had happened following his return to the UK the first time he visited San Antonio. Watching the DVDs of the services he'd attended that weekend with his mother and continuing to admire Maria in the choir segments, he pointed her out and said, "I'm gonna marry that girl!"

He never thought anything of it. All he thought he meant by what he said was that he was going to marry someone *like* that girl—someone whose heart was for the Lord and who had a beautiful smile that could light up a room. His mother didn't take him seriously at the time, and neither did he. Now, faced with a date with her and linked to his first thoughts about marrying the next girl he dated, he was starting to become more anxious.

Lastly, he remembered Columbus, Ohio. The word "WIFE" written on the donation envelope was in full view inside his head every time he closed his eyes. In the end he simply smiled and prayed, "Well, Lord, if this is to be, then You've got a whole lot of work ahead of You!"

Finally Sunday morning arrived. When he woke up, Jim reached for the nicotine gum he brought with him for the plane instead of his customary cigarette. It wouldn't calm his nerves as much as the cigarettes, but at least he'd smell better before his date. Also, Maria didn't strike him as the kind of girl who smoked, so he decided to keep his habit from her to begin with. Anyway, his New Year resolution was to stop smoking on July first, and this was June first, so one more month and he'd be smoke-free, and she'd never need to know. *Hiding things from her already, eh? Great way to start a 'relationship' Jimmy boy!*

Church started at 8:30 a.m. and lasted until around 10:00 a.m., and then a second service began at 11:00 a.m. As a choir member,

Maria was obligated to stay for both services until her singing duties finished midway through the second, and then she would be free to meet up for lunch. While she performed in the first, Jim studied her intently from his seat a few rows from the front of the stage, his heart pounding and his head somewhat adrift from the main reason he was in church in the first place—to praise God. Maria didn't seem to have any problems remembering where she was; she was shining like never before as she sang, and all at once feelings of inferiority began to accompany Jim's existing feelings of nervousness and confusion. *How could someone who appeared to be so angelic ever end up being interested in someone so messed up as me?* he thought. It didn't seem feasible to him, and soon his nerves were fading with his hopes as he prematurely wrote off his chances and began to relax.

He spent the time in between services in the church's extensive bookshop while Steve and Diane were performing duties elsewhere. Just as he was about to purchase a book, Steve came running and grabbed him by the shoulder.

"Hey, do you wanna meet her now?" he asked.

"Ehhh. Aye, I suppose! Where?"

"Quick, put the book down and come with me. She's not got much time before she has to go backstage and get ready to sing again. I told her you were dying to meet her, so she said she'd hang around for a bit," Steve said as they took off in a hurry.

"Dying to meet her" was not the condition Jim found himself in when Steve came running since he still hadn't come up with an opening line for when he met her yet! "Flustered and terrified" was a more apt description!

They rounded the corner, and there was Maria walking in their direction. It was the first time Jim had seen her without her choir robes on, but when she smiled as she saw them coming towards her, there was no doubt it was her—her smile was unmistakable.

"Hey Maria, how ye doin'?"

"Good!" she beamed.

"Aye, Steve said ye'd be up for some lunch with us. That's pure great! I just told him once that I thought ye looked great when ye were singin,' and he thought it would be great if we went for some lunch. It's great that ye want to come with us after yer done singin'!" Jim went on, his Scottish accent accentuated and quickened by nerves. Maria's happy expression turned to bewilderment.

"We'll meet you out here after you're finished singing," Steve said in translation.

"Sure!" Maria said, her smile returning.

"So ye've got to go sing again?" Jim asked the obvious, knowing full-well what the answer would be.

"Yeah."

"Och aye, see ye after then!"

And that was that. Their first meeting was over inside a minute, and Jim instantly began replaying it over in his mind as he walked with Steve back in the opposite direction. More self-criticism and deprecation followed as he began wishing he'd said no to Steve's request to meet her ahead of time.

"So do you still like her?" Steve asked.

"Oh, aye!" Jim replied emphatically.

Even though their first meeting didn't go anywhere near as well as Jim would've liked, the lunch date still went ahead. Maria brought along her twelve-year-old son, Isaac, and Steve and Diane accompanied Jim. Jim continued his less-than-perfect first impressions by ordering a bloody twenty-ounce T-bone steak with all the trimmings and then a large dessert, both of which he finished without trace. Maria sat next to him, trying her best not to wince too much at the blood on Jim's plate.

Aside from the nerves, overeating, talking too fast, and constantly thinking of cigarettes, the first "date" seemed to Jim to go well. This was the first time Steve and Diane had properly met with Maria, so they helped out by keeping the conversation going throughout. Any time Jim started off a conversation, it was usually about how things were different in the UK or a vague one about nothing in particular in order not to tip anyone off that he was still on edge at being in Maria's presence. His conversations usually took longer to complete, too, since most of the time anything he said had to be re-translated into Texas-English as a result of her difficulty in understanding his Scottish dialect. He later thought that if the whole scene had been videoed and edited for content, then he'd probably find he didn't end up saying much at all!

The lunch date finished, they went their separate ways with no follow-up arranged—no exchange of phone numbers, addresses or e-mails or plans to meet up again. Jim thought to himself, *Ah well, that was nice, but hey-ho!* He was due to leave to go back to the UK the next day anyway and had no plans to come back to Texas for another five months, so reminding himself of the practicalities of the situation helped him overcome his disappointment that he probably wouldn't get to see her again except to just say hello the next time he came over. Upon returning to Steve and Diane's house, he immediately smoked two cigarettes as he sat by himself in the garden reflecting on how he might've done the whole thing different if he had the chance to do it again. He began pondering, too, the build-up to the event and all his conversations with God. Finally, in order to rescue his belief that God still answered prayers, he came to the conclusion that Maria was not a date and, therefore, his old prayer regarding the one he'd marry still stood. The disappointment was still painful though.

He decided not to go to church in the evening, choosing instead to go into the heart of San Antonio with Steve and Diane to take a boat ride down the river. Steve had asked Maria at lunch if she wanted to join them, but she declined, stating choir duties at church as her reason not to come. However legitimate her reason was, Jim still saw it as a snub.

The trip downtown was enjoyable, but he couldn't stop thinking about Maria. When they returned to the house Steve disappeared into another room with the telephone while Jim talked with Diane in the kitchen as she cleaned up. All he wanted to do was go to bed with his depression and be done with the socializing for the day, but he decided to wait for Steve to come off the phone before he said goodnight. Steve seemed to be taking forever with the call until finally he came through to the kitchen with the phone.

"Hey, do you want to talk to Maria?" he asked Jim, handing him the phone.

"Aye, too right! I didn't know that's who you were talking to!" Jim replied, immediately abandoning the gloom that had surrounded him all evening.

Steve covered the mouthpiece of the phone and quickly filled Jim in with snippets of information he'd just learned in his conversation with Maria that he thought might be of use to him. He'd found out that Maria's previous husband had passed away at a young age eight years ago and that she wasn't a fan of hanging out in bars. Armed with this information (although not sure what to do with it), he took the phone and disappeared into the bedroom.

He managed to slow his speech down enough for them to have a decent conversation this time. Maria told of how much she'd enjoyed her time at lunch, and Jim apologized for being a glutton. She spoke of how wonderful the church service was that evening, and he spoke of how he wished he'd now come too. And she asked if he had any plans to settle in America at any point in the future. Jim responded by giving her a long rundown on the various options available in order for an individual to immigrate to the United States. In New Orleans, he'd researched all the ways to immigrate as a way of using up the remainder of his prepaid-Internet time at the library, so the information was fresh in his memory as he reeled it off with authority. In closing, however, he pointed out that none of the options were feasible to him before eventually answering her question with, "No."

"I'd still *like* to," he continued. "But it'd take an almighty miracle for it to happen!"

"Well, if it's what you want," Maria responded, "I'll believe with you in faith that God will bring it to pass."

"Thank you, that'd be great!"

He hadn't previously given much thought to moving to America before—sure it would be nice, but it wasn't high on his wish list—until now, that was. He suddenly felt himself falling in love with Maria. A thorough review of the rules would now be called for just in case he'd missed anything. He knew at this point that he wouldn't be returning to America for another five months, and his mind drifted as he tried to think if he could manage another visit in between.

"I'd like to keep in touch with you. Do y'all use e-mail?" Maria asked, bringing him back into the present.

"Aye, do you want my address?"

"I'll give you mine. Do you have a pen?"

Jim wrote Maria's e-mail address on the back of a till receipt he found in his back pocket, then placed it inside the book he was reading at the time. It was to become his regular bookmark so that every time he read, he would get to think of Maria.

The conversation ended on a promise that he would write to Maria once he got back to the UK. He returned to Steve and Diane in the kitchen, brandishing the e-mail address to them as if it were a trophy he'd just won.

"Do you think y'all will keep in touch?" Diane asked.

"I sure hope so!" Jim replied emphatically. "*I* certainly will!"

Chapter Four

Upon returning to the UK Jim headed straight for his mother's house where he unpacked his bags. He came across the book he was reading on the plane with the receipt sticking out—the one with Maria's e-mail address written on it—then spent the rest of the day trying to formulate in his head what he would say in his first message to her that evening. Once he finally sat down, he started off:

> Hey Maria, how ye doin'?

He wrote a few lines thanking her for agreeing to meet with him and for calling on the Sunday night. Then he decided to let her know the main reason for wanting to meet with her:

> I wanted to say thank you for being such an inspiration. It was seeing you worship that first caught my attention: I can't remember seeing as much passion and joy overflowing in a person in the presence of Jesus as what you have, and you seem to just light up with love for Him. It's something I know can't be taught but I wish I could express myself as you do (I also wish I could sing! Nicely, I mean!). It was for those reasons I wanted to meet you as I think you have something special in that respect. I'm glad I did get to meet you and, again, thank you.

It was quite a bold paragraph for a first e-mail, and he finished off by saying how he hoped he hadn't made her self-conscious and how he hoped she'd drop him a line from time to time. He prayed over the e-mail, asking God to bless it, then tentatively hit the send button. Afterwards he went to bed, but despite his tiredness, it took him a long while to get to sleep. He played back the whole e-mail in his head over and over as well as wondered when, or if, she'd reply. To his great delight, there was a reply waiting for him the very next morning.

He grinned his way through every word of her message! Once he'd finished reading it, he looked up to heaven and said out loud, "Thank You! Thank You! Thank You! Thank You! Thank You!" Then he went back to the start and re-read it many times over. It wasn't a small message simply thanking him for his, either; it was a full page giving him more snippets of information about herself as well as her response to his comments on her worshipping style. As he might've expected, it was full of humility:

> As far as being an inspiration to you, PRAISE GOD…I do believe the Lord has given me a gift to sing and the pleasure of singing. I don't know that I sing "nicely," although when I'm in the midst of others, I sing okay. My walk with the Lord has become so sweet in the last couple of years that now that I know the words to the songs, the words minister to me when I sing them. This is my personal way to express my love for my Lord. To just "sing" the words is a waste of time. I think about how "we are all going to be accountable for the words we say," so I choose to sing the words with meaning and love, and that's how I come across. I am so happy to be used by the Lord in this respect.…

The grin that accompanied his reading of Maria's message stayed with him the whole day! His mind was preoccupied with her sweet words as well as his own ideas of what he was going to say in return. And also the timing of his reply—*Should I reply that same day or wait a day or two so as not to appear too eager?* he wondered. In the end he figured that since adhering in the past to common dating rules never did him any good, he would abandon them and reply right away. Once again that night he prayed over his e-mail before sending it, and once again Maria replied straight away.

In the days that followed, the e-mails bounced back and forth with neither Jim nor Maria wanting to be the one to break the flow. For the first couple of weeks, the e-mails remained light-hearted and full of facts about each other's respective lives and characters. Then subtle hints of a potentially deeper relationship began to emerge as the writing grew longer and more meaningful in its content. Only a lingering reminder of the physical distance that separated them was enough to keep it simple. *After all, what could possibly happen to allow this to work? Only a miracle!* Jim thought.

Back at work, Jim began telling his colleagues of his new friend. New relationships were commonplace in the airline industry, especially among flight attendants; therefore, seldom did anyone pay particular attention to the latest couple in existence. Yet for some reason, the news of Jim's story was attracting a lot of interest as his workmates became hungry to hear the next daily installment and would excitedly question him about it as soon as he walked through the door. He tried to play down the existence of any romance, but the way in which he'd gush about Maria together with the smile that would erupt on his face each time her name was mentioned made it difficult to convince anyone that he was only interested in her friendship.

On the other side of the ocean, Maria was experiencing similar interest. Her friends and colleagues were also aware of her single-status and were beginning to see a change. Her regular cheeriness was heightened, her smile became even more prominent than usual, and her willingness to share her new-found knowledge of all-things British were becoming a regular part of conversation. By nature she was not one to allow herself to get carried away, but for some reason, this felt different. She was desperate to find out more and each night would speed home from work and head straight for the computer where an e-mail from Jim would inevitably be waiting.

Maria recognized the deep devotion to God that existed in Jim. The years in which he had spent trying to quench it were over, and now his daily appreciation of God's grace in keeping him alive was all too apparent to her. Even his early revelations of his wayward history could not deter her. It was obvious that he was only looking forward now and would continue to move in that direction. With Maria's encouraging words to help him along, he was becoming stronger, too.

Jim continued to pray for the miracle that might make it possible for him and Maria to be together on a regular basis. He looked for employment in various other airlines that would allow him stopovers in San Antonio but to no avail. He researched Texas universities to see whether he might be taken on as a foreign student, but the cost was too great. He even investigated the criteria required for starting up a business in America, but again it would prove too difficult. Soon afterwards, his hopes were raised when, Kevin—a friend he had made on his first visit to San Antonio—wrote and said he would look into obtaining a job for him at his company. Kevin held a top position in the field of energy resource and generator manufacturing and mentioned that his firm often employed overseas individuals and assisted them in obtaining their visas. Even though Jim knew nothing of this industry, he was still willing to study and do all it took to get into it. The excitement that this might be the opening he needed stayed with him for three weeks until Kevin ultimately broke the news that he was unable to help after all. Disappointed, but undeterred, he continued to press on in his belief that if indeed God wanted for him and Maria to be together, then, however impossible it may be, He would still make a way.

Often in his role as senior flight attendant, Jim would take time out to entertain the passengers by cracking jokes and generally making light of their flying experience over the PA system. This approach won him many complimentary letters and company recognition awards, but on this one occasion, it won him the attention of a female passenger traveling alone and sitting directly across from him in her front-row seat.

Without doubt, she was extremely attractive. She spoke with a South American accent, her skin was tanned, and her hair was long and dark. She stylishly wore a short skirt, sheer dark hose, and knee-length boots. Shiny pink lip-gloss and large hoop earrings completed her look. She was the type of woman that Jim had, for many years, fantasized his future partner would look like. During the flight she informed his colleagues that she lived in London, she was available, and on top of it all, she was interested in him.

Knowing of his long-distance correspondence with Maria and that it was non-romantic in nature, Jim's colleagues tried to convince him to go for it with this girl.

"We think you should!" they said.

"No, it's not fair to Maria," he replied. After all, he, too, knew that there was no existing love affair between him and Maria, and only his faith in God at this point was keeping the chances of it actually becoming one alive.

"But you're not 'going out' with her! Besides, even if you were, she lives in America, and she won't ever find out! Just go—what have you got to lose?" one of them said.

That last argument, with all its weight, only succeeded in turning Jim's attention in the opposite direction. If a relationship with Maria ever were to become reality, he knew that she *would* find out, because he would tell her! His honesty, in addition to his guilt, would compel him to. Besides that, he knew of another couple whose relationship began in exactly the same way. After they had first met, one of the pair had embarked on a brief fling with a third party before the partnership was fully established. It was to prove a continuous and constant sorrow in their union and contributed to the eventual demise of their marriage. There was no way Jim wanted to take that chance with Maria, however slim the likelihood of being together was, and so he informed his colleagues he would not be taking up this girl's offer of a date. Even as the plane came into land, the girl herself asked him directly for his phone number, but he simply smiled an apologetic no in return. The other crew members were incredulous, including the pilots who were watching and drooling over the girl from their cockpit windows as she walked to the terminal; however, a strange feeling inside let him know he'd done the right thing.

He didn't tell Maria what happened in his e-mail to her that night. For all his satisfaction in staying loyal to a potential relationship with her, he still couldn't help hearing voices in his head questioning his decision. The next day however, there was a bonus message from Maria in addition to her regular e-mail, which read,

> Just a short note to tell you thanks for the e-mails. I know you don't have to send me an e-mail back every time I send one to you, but your thoughts edify me and lift me up. And I truly enjoy reading and writing. I thank you for your friendship!!! You seem like a God-fearing man and a very respectful gentleman. Thanks again!! I just hope I do the same for you ...smiles and blessings.
>
> Maria

It wasn't an outright confession of love, but to Jim, it certainly felt like it! A sweet and oh-so-timely message from a sweet lady that reminded him of why he was hanging on so desperately to the slim chance that they might one day end up together. It was all he needed to erase the memory of the girl on the plane and fully concentrate again on Maria.

As the e-mails continued to flow, the two increasingly shared information about themselves. Jim learned a great deal about Maria's extensive family, her three children, and how she spent many years raising them alone. Maria in turn learned of Jim's troubled past, his addiction to alcohol, and his ongoing addiction to cigarettes. He was surprised to find out she was ten years older than he was as she looked so incredibly young. She was surprised to hear of his limited education as his discernible intelligence suggested otherwise. What was most surprising to them both was that they shared the same birthday! In the first month of writing to each other, they both suffered setbacks in their personal lives—Maria's mother required invasive hospital treatment, and Jim had to deal with the loss of a friend, and neither were willing to hold back or be afraid to let the other know the full extent of their emotions in each situation. Every e-mail contained references to God as they shared their growing faith with each other, and interspersed in all their communications were small clues that the infatuation Jim had for Maria was not all one-way. In another e-mail she wrote,

> Thank you for your friendship Jim. I know I've said it before but you are different (in a positive way, again). I feel close to you (even miles away) just by the same faith and love for God we share. I like the fact that I can come to you for prayer, and I know that you will pray and are just as excited or more for me when prayers are answered. Like we are doing right now...that's why I like you and thank you. I thank God for you, too, Jim, for I know God gives us the desires of our hearts. I have been praising, worshipping, serving, and trying to further His Kingdom in one way or another, and then He broadsided me with you!

About the time he received this e-mail Jim decided he *had* to make another trip to San Antonio even if it was just for a day!

Jim's best friend, Darius, also worked in aviation as a manager for a larger airline. His employment allowed him one return flight per year for himself and a traveling companion to any destination of his choice. It so happened that Darius had time off work coming up and was debating whether or not to make use of his free flights when Jim decided to give him a call.

Darius was, in many people's opinions, the nicest guy alive. He was kind and compassionate, soft-spoken and timid, a giant of a man yet always the first to run from trouble, and, above all, a devoted Christian. He was ten years older than Jim, and they had first met when he taught his junior Sunday school class when Jim was only ten. As the years went by and Jim reached adulthood, they became friends, and as he descended into self-destruction, Darius followed from a distance. He had rescued him from many desperate situations during the years of his alcoholic confinement and stood by him until his eventual escape. His generosity knew no limits, and Jim knew he never had to hesitate in asking him for a favor.

"Have you decided where you're gonna take me with your free tickets yet?" Jim asked sarcastically.

"No, not yet. Why? I thought you didn't have any more time off work until October?"

"I don't, but I might be able to swing an extra day or two onto my regular days off, and we could make a long weekend of it."

"Did *you* have anywhere in mind?" Darius asked suspiciously, knowing Jim no doubt had a hidden agenda.

"I thought…and don't worry if you're not up for it…it's just an idea…but I was just wondering…why don't we go to San Antonio? We could go to the big church I keep telling you about. We could stay with my good friends Steve and Diane, so we wouldn't need to worry about accommodation costs or taxi fares. You could see the Alamo and the Riverwalk. You could meet Maria. It'll be nice and hot. I'll pay for it."

"Aye, okay. What dates?"

"Eh?"

"I said 'aye, okay.' What dates did you have in mind?"

For a second Jim was caught off-guard at the ease of Darius's persuading. Here Darius had the chance to go anywhere in the world, and yet he was content to make it San Antonio, where Jim had already been three times before. Whether it was the overwhelming sales pitch that did it or the offer of a free vacation, it didn't matter now—Jim was halfway there, and all he needed to do now was get the time off work.

Complex rules within the aviation industry meant that flight attendants could obtain spare days where they were not required to fly but still counted as duty. Such days, however, had several restrictions on them that prevented them from being classed as days off, and they could be changed at any time at the company's discretion, even the night before. They could not be relied upon, and no one ever made advance plans to do anything in them. With careful manipulation and inside help, they could, at best, be made favorable but never taken for granted.

Jim took a leap of faith. He had two spare days, which he sweet-talked a company manager into switching to tag onto either side of his regular three days off. He then had Darius book the seats and spent the next week constantly monitoring his spare days to make sure they didn't change. He wrote and told Maria he was coming, and his bags were packed in anticipation. Above all, he prayed continuously.

Sure enough, his prayers were answered. The night before his departure for Texas, he finished work, checked his rota for the final time, and found that it was still the same. It was the height of the summer—the airline's busiest time of year—and no one else ever seemed to get any favors, yet even so, God came through for him and ensured he got to keep those two precious extra days off. They could not be changed now. Four hours later he was on the bus to the airport with Darius and with a huge smile on his face; he was going to see Maria again!

In Texas they were met by Steve and Diane, who welcomed them into their home. Despite being worn out from the long journey, they stayed up late as Darius became acquainted with his new hosts, and Jim tried hard to ensure he would be tired enough to sleep through the jetlag. He had given up smoking four days previously, which also made sleeping difficult, but ultimately it was the thoughts of what he would say to Maria the next day that kept him awake most of the night.

The following day after church, they met up with her and her oldest son, Ricardo, and went to a steakhouse nearby. Jim sat down next to Maria, and still under the illusion that women were impressed by a man with a large capacity for food, he again proceeded to order the largest steak on the menu, devour it all, and follow it with a dessert! No matter how nervous he was, at any given time, his large appetite remained constant.

Yes, he was nervous, although he wasn't sure why. He had learned a lot about Maria from her e-mails, which should have given him plenty to talk to her about, yet now he found himself struggling for words. He already knew that it was still too early to say, "I love you." Maybe it was because his e-mails were so eloquent and he didn't want to disappoint in real-life discourse when he spoke. Or perhaps it was just the fact that he felt he was being watched more closely than the last time—Darius already knew that Jim's interest in Maria was romantic, and Steve and Diane were not convinced, either, that he wanted to keep their relationship platonic. Ricardo seemed untroubled by his mother's new-found companion, or else he hid his suspicion well. Maria, too, was feeling the same scrutiny and was similarly quiet at first.

As with their first lunch together, Steve and Diane were happy to keep the dialogue going, and Darius delighted in contributing embarrassing stories of when Jim was in his junior Sunday school class. Jim retorted with some stories of his own about Darius until Steve stepped in to re-direct their extended conversation when it became exclusive of everyone else at the table. Diane questioned Maria about choir while Ricardo had everyone fascinated with details of his university research. It was an enjoyable experience and another seemingly successful liaison. When it was over, Jim gave Maria a hug, careful not to invade too much of her personal space and give the others too much to read into. Even so, in that small moment of physical contact, he felt like he'd taken another step deeper into her world.

That same night she came round to Steve and Diane's house where they sat up playing cards until midnight, and the next day she met with Steve, Darius, and Jim to embark on a trip to downtown San Antonio. On each occasion Jim was relatively quiet and surprised at himself at how much distance he put between them both. They'd spent so much time discussing their lives by e-mail, yet here they were, together in person, and he was struggling to engage her. He knew he was already in love with her, but the geographical complications of confessing his love persisted in his head. Trying to steer his head onto other matters proved too difficult, and, as such, he let the others do most of the talking until they parted company a final time that evening with another genial hug.

"Are you still happy to keep e-mailing me?" he asked in closing.

"Sure," she replied softly yet unconvincingly.

The remainder of the day, he tried to stay upbeat for the sake of his hosts and for Darius, but it wasn't long before he slipped into despondent quietness. Soon afterwards, dejected by his behavior and overwhelmed by the practicalities of a seemingly impossible relationship, he excused himself and went to bed early. There he prayed, "Well, I guess nothing's gonna happen after all, Lord. I really hoped this would be the time where I'd find out for sure if anything could come of us being together, but again I'm left with nothing. I know You're a God of the impossible, but all I keep getting is 'Not this time!' When is it ever gonna be my time? We had so much to say in the e-mails, and yet today I could hardly talk to her. What's that all about? Ah, well, at least I tried. And at least I'll have one more person I'll know when I come over in October again with the family. I guess, thank You for letting me know early before I got my hopes up any more. And thank You for giving me and Darius a good time while we were here. In Jesus's name. Amen."

It was hardly a prayer of reverence, but such was the way he was feeling. It was almost like he didn't care. Even though none of this was God's fault, he was intent on blaming Him in an attempt to justify his feelings. *How could God allow me to get so far down the line with this woman, knowing full-well how I feel about her? It's almost like a sick joke!*

Eventually he fell asleep. In the morning he awoke to find Darius already dressed and reading his Bible.

"Morning!" said Darius.

"Mm!" Jim grumbled, still half-asleep.

"I had a weird dream. Do you want to hear it? It had you in it. I think you'll like it!"

"Uh, okay."

"I was on a skateboard ..."

This in itself was enough to cheer Jim up! Darius's oversize physique was often the subject of his jokes, and to picture him on a skateboard was side-splittingly funny!

"Sounds like a nightmare! For you, I mean! Was I there to see it?" Jim asked, laughing.

"Like I was saying," Darius continued, ignoring Jim's amusement at his opening statement. "I was on a skateboard in an art gallery whizzing by various paintings. It was as if I was seeing into my future in these paintings, as they all depicted events that are going to happen in the upcoming months and years. The thing is, I only saw the first picture clearly as all the rest were blurred, but do you want to know what I saw?"

"What?"

"It was you getting married, and I was there to see it."

"Was I marrying Maria?" Jim asked excitedly—and selfishly—somewhat disinterested in what Darius's dream could have meant for him personally.

"I *think* so. Your bride had long dark hair, anyway, so it *could*'ve been her."

"Cool! What else?"

"Well, that's all I can remember. I got such a shock at the first painting that I didn't really pay any attention to the other ones. And they were all going by so fast. But then I asked the Lord about it, and first of all, He told me '*Little by little!*'"

"Little by little" was a teaching point raised by the pastor in his sermon in the Sunday morning service they had attended two days earlier. He quoted it from Deuteronomy 7:22. On Monday morning Darius read it again during his own regular morning Bible study in the book of Exodus, so it was certainly appropriate and somewhat non-coincidental that he should be reminded of it again on Tuesday. Jim had taken great heart from the pastor's sermon that Sunday, believing it was definitely intended by God for him to hear. When Darius shared his study with him on Monday, it further boosted his confidence, yet somehow the events of the day seemed to drain it away again. Now hearing it for a third time in three days definitely seemed like God was saying something, and his mood was lifted further.

"Go on!" said Jim.

"He told me to say to you that you are to tell Maria how you really feel about her and that you shouldn't wait too long to do it. He also told me to tell you that you're not to ever think she's too good for you either."

"But…you saw how it went yesterday! Nothing happened, and it didn't seem like anything *could* happen either! Plus I'm not gonna see her again for another three and a half months! Why didn't He tell you all this yesterday before we went out? That way I might've told her then! How am I supposed to say it to her now? How 'not too long' is 'not too long'?"

"I-I-I don't know," Darius stuttered apologetically. "'Little by little' I suppose!"

"Is that it—is that all you heard?"

"Uh-huh. Sorry, mate."

Jim trusted Darius completely when it came to hearing from God, and now his emotions were alternating between elation and confusion. Darius had a good track record in this area, so Jim was pretty confident that he had heard correct. The lack of specifics, however, were causing turmoil, and as he subsequently redirected his countless questions to God in the shower, the same three words kept echoing in his own head: "*Little by little!*"

Chapter Five

Maria sat down at the computer and glanced at the clock. Right now Jim was on a plane on his way back to the UK, and a feeling of anti-climax had taken hold of her. The short period of time she would get to spend with him was now officially over—the second chance to establish in her mind just *why* exactly she had spent a whole month writing to him—and it had gone by so quickly it seemed like it hadn't taken place at all.

A smile came to her face as she recalled various events of the weekend and how much fun she'd had. As she began typing her e-mail to Jim and making references to those events, an opinion began to form in her head that maybe overall, it was just simply that—fun. There were no hints from Jim at a romance, no gestures or physical contact from which she could construe that his intentions were otherwise different from amity. She wondered whether continuing the e-mails at the same depth as before was worth it. It was nice, but would it ultimately prove fruitless? After all, he had no plans to move nearby soon, nor did he have much hope of doing so either. Why was she doing this again?

Finally she considered the fact that it would be over three months before she would see Jim again, and to continue corresponding on just a general level until that time would be quite a obligation, one to which she was unsure she could commit. Not wanting to upset things between them, however, she concluded her e-mail by saying she would continue to write but that her messages would be a lot shorter in future. Maybe by simply keeping the dialogue thin, the lack of gratification from it would cause things to drift away on their own she reasoned.

Content that she had made the correct decision, she confidently hit send, turned off her computer, and went to bed. The following day she continued to try to convince herself she was doing the right thing in not allowing herself to become any more involved; however, since she wasn't exactly sure why she did so in the first place, her thoughts of the whole situation were proving difficult to lay to rest. In order to find some sort of peace inside her head, she ultimately resolved to wait and see what Jim's response would be and take it from there.

When she got home from work, there was a very long and excitable e-mail from Jim waiting in her inbox. It explained in great detail his return journey, all he had done since he'd got home, how much he enjoyed his time in San Antonio, and how he still believed God might allow him to live there one day. In addition, there were more divulgences of personal information, all of which suggested that either he hadn't fully picked up on the hint that he too should keep his messages short and light, or he had disregarded it. In an attempt to re-establish her position, she sent him an even shorter message that evening.

In actual fact Jim *had* deduced her withdrawal. He'd been on the receiving end of retractions from relationships in the past and was experienced at reading the signs. Under normal circumstances he would've assumed a position of retreat until the final blow was inevitably delivered—continue at a distance until it was eventually pronounced over. This time, however, he was determined it was going to be different. He decided to throw off his feelings of negativity and resolved he was going to give God the benefit of the doubt and trust Him that his prayers were still being answered. Buoyed by Darius's dream and words of encouragement, he knew he had a fighting chance at keeping things going, and he vowed not to give up. The e-mails he sent over the next three nights continued in a similar vein—long and full of personal disclosure.

Bemused, Maria reflected on her decision to try to free herself from it all and began questioning God instead. By this point she knew she now had feelings for Jim but, like him, had no idea what to do with them. Similarly, she knew that if she were to ever end up in a relationship with him that God would have to provide a way for it to happen. She knew He *could*; she just wasn't sure if He *would*.

That same weekend, the church was holding an overnight stay for its single-parent members at its country retreat. There would be no distractions of everyday life, no phone signal or Internet, just a chance for those parents and their children to spend the night with others in fun and fellowship or enjoy some solitude amid the Texas hills. Maria had planned to attend the event for a while, and now it could not have come at a better time. Before she left, she prayed that God would speak to her while she was there and let her know what to do with regard to the whole Jim situation.

On the other side of the ocean, Jim was asking God to do the same. He was already semi-confident that a relationship with Maria had been authorized, but since she was not yet aware of that fact, he wondered how he was going to tell her. "Y'know, it would be so much easier if You told her ahead of me!" he told God.

Maria was leaving straight from work to go to the retreat, so there was no need to send her a message that evening. Jim took advantage of his night off by tidying up The Shoebox, which had been severely neglected in recent weeks as a result of all the e-mailing. As he worked he spent the whole time listening to music and chatting to God. "Lord, if You could please just speak to her while she's away tonight. Let her know how I feel about her. I don't know how You're gonna do that, mind You. Maybe You could have someone else say something to her that might trigger something in her head that might make her go 'Aha, that's what this is all about!' And then she'll come home certain in her head that she likes me in the same way I like her. I know there's so much more to think of beyond that, but right now this is all that matters. I just want her to know that I love her. I know I'm the one who has to make that first move. I want to tell her, I really do! I just don't want to be disappointed at her response. I need You to prepare her heart for me. I need to be 110 percent sure she'll be receptive to me. If You could give me just one more sign too, that'd be great."

Right then his wedding song randomly began playing on the stereo! This was the song he decided would be the one to which he'd like to dance with his bride (whomever she may be) at their wedding, should he ever get married. He'd even considered learning how to play it on the piano so that he could surprise her by singing it to her at the reception. Actually *marrying* Maria was not in his mind right then, but to hear that exact song at that precise moment in time just as he'd finished asking God for a sign was enough for him to know that God had just answered him. It was proof that God was interested, and his eyes filled up with tears of joy.

Meanwhile, in Texas, Maria stole some time to be by herself and wandered alongside the river. She sat down by a dam and sang softly to herself as a solitary fish stared up at her from the water. Surrounded by nature with no one else around, she began singing louder praise songs to God. Just being in the countryside with all its beauty and wildlife and a feeling of closeness to God was enough to bring peace to her thoughts and a smile to her face.

She ambled her way to the main building where food was being served, and her friend Julie had kept her a seat. Julie had noticed a change in Maria's demeanor of late and was curious to know why. As Maria began telling the story of Jim from Scotland, Julie erupted in gleeful excitement. She was of Scottish descent, and Maria couldn't stop laughing as she continued the rest of the conversation in her best Scottish accent.

"Och aye, so he's a wee Scottish laddie, eh? And does he have his own kilt?" Julie asked with glee.

"Umm, yeah."

"Och, that's great! And is he gonna be movin' over here?"

"I don't know. I know he'd like to, but it's difficult."

"Och aye, I'm sure he will. If it's meant to be, it'll be!"

Julie saw a positive side in everything and loved to share her enthusiasm with whomever she talked to. Making people happy was one of her favorite pastimes, and she always had an encouraging word even if she didn't have all the answers. As she began to settle down, she could tell Maria was looking for guidance, and at that point something in her let her know what to say.

"I think you should," she said confidently.

"What?"

"Just be open to it. Trust God and let Him do the rest."

A smile formed on Maria's face. Julie's words felt like they had been spoken to her by God Himself, and she knew she had just received the confirmation for which she'd been praying at home the day before. As she drove home later that day, she couldn't wait to write to Jim and tell him all about her weekend. The message she eventually did send him was vibrant and full of joy, and it was clear to Jim that she was excited about something.

She didn't recount the exact details of her conversation with Julie but mentioned that she had received confirmation from God of something that had been on her heart. In his reply Jim expressed his delight that she'd heard from God but stopped short of asking her outright what it was, hoping she might volunteer the information in her next message. She didn't. The following evening she again made reference to the fact that she'd received an answer to prayer but kept the details silent. Still on a high, however, she wrote,

> I never told you that in March, at the picnic, Steve came running over to me, while I was walking with my niece, and he asked me, "Are you married?" I had seen him before at church, but never really had met him. So I start looking around for cameras because now I think I'm on "Candid Camera" or something. I told him, "No, no I'm not." Then he said, "Good, because I know someone in Scotland who's in love with you and wants to meet you." (He actually said that, I'm not making that up). I looked puzzled, "How does he know me?" He says, "He sees you on TV in the choir." I agreed, and he told me you would be coming down in October, so we could get together then. I walked a little taller that afternoon, knowing someone thought I was special enough to come and visit me while he was in town all the way from Scotland. As I walked away, I was still looking for cameras in the trees or on the light poles or something. Later I passed by a booth where he and Diane were working, and I met her at that time. So that place is special to me for a lot of reasons.

Jim's heart galloped as he read her words. He knew the time was now! Something inside him told him that his reply would *have* to contain that defining moment when he would tell Maria he was in love with her!

He spent the whole day preoccupied with what he was going to say, and since he didn't have to go to work, he had plenty of time to think about it. Yet, as the day wore on, the more afraid he became. Despite all the prophetic words and reassurances he'd received up until now, doubts were starting to creep in, and he tried to justify various ways in which he could back out. Even as he limped precariously into his message at 10:25 p.m., he started by apologizing in advance that his message might be short on account of the time. It was no use. He just couldn't see how he was going to do it!

Six large, general paragraphs later, he slumped back in his chair as feelings of disgust at his own cowardice began to overtake him. He put both hands over his face and rubbed his forehead back and forward. As he removed his hands and his eyes began to re-focus, he turned to see his Bible on the bed with the program from the church service he'd attended in San Antonio the week before sticking out. The program gave a synopsis of the pastor's sermon, and it concluded,

> For those of you looking for a spiritual breakthrough, understand that the final step into a land flowing with milk and honey will be your most courageous step. Will you take it? Or will you live in mediocrity for the balance of your life in the wilderness?

All of a sudden, a surge of strength came over him as the intense words seemed to hit him with overpowering force. He turned his eyes back to the computer and furiously resumed typing. The words were now flowing freely, and, without once going back to correct a sentence, he wrote,

> It's true that when I saw you in the choir, I was instantly attracted to you. I checked it out with God that it wasn't a physical or looks thing and straight away knew that it wasn't. I'd heard that love at first sight in its general sense was not something Christians should entertain since you didn't know the person just from looking at them, thereby technically re-classifying it as nearer to lust. However, I knew that with you I was in love with the Jesus you display, and that was pouring out from every part of your being. That's what I wanted to get close to when I said I wanted to meet you. I just don't think I got that point across to Steve as fully as I might've!
>
> But moving on…I do feel I have to now let you know that now I feel like I am actually in love with you both as a person

> as well as someone who is full of the glory of Jesus but separately at the same time (if that makes sense?) I don't know if that's something you wanted to hear, whether it puts things between us into a whole different atmosphere either in a bad or good sense. I've been praying that the latter is the case…I just know that I'm in agreement with you that we complement each other and make a great team. If God wants us to be together in person, then I know He'll find a way. If He doesn't, I'll keep on believing and trusting in Him regardless. I, like you, always want God to be number one in my life. I know one thing—and on this point I'll leave it til I hear from you again—I've never encountered *anyone* in this whole world who is as special as you are; not just to me, but to everyone I talk to about you.

Exhausted and drained, he brought his message to a close and went back and re-read it several times. He formulated in his mind every possible way in which Maria could reply and already began considering each counter-response. Again he thought about abandoning the whole thing, but this time he was able to quickly cast those thoughts aside, now confident the time was right. As the clock turned 12:15 a.m., he tentatively stretched out his hand to the computer screen and prayed over his message. Finally, he hit send and watched it disappear. As he closed his eyes and exhaled deeply, the words he had just typed replayed over and over in his head and continued to do so as he made his way into bed. Three hours later his thoughts, at last, gave way to sleep.

A further three hours later, he awoke again. Immediately he turned on his computer. His heart rate was already in overdrive, and his body was seemingly unaware of only having had three hours sleep. Excitement and panic were interchangeable as he first speculated what Maria's reply might be then wondered if there would be a message waiting for him at all. All the while, the Internet was taking longer than ever to start up (or so it felt)!

Eventually his e-mail list came into view. At the very top there was indeed a message from Maria, the title of which read,

> The feeling's mutual!

Jim threw his hands up in the air in celebration. He laughed victoriously and began pumping the air with his fists. If he had been capable of doing backflips, he would've done a few right there and then! Without even opening the e-mail, he began praising God in his usual way when he was excited: "Thank You! Thank You! Thank You! Thank You! Thank You!" Eventually, elation gave way to relief, which in turn brought relative calm enough to read the rest of the message. Maria wrote,

> Thank you for your last message. It was the double top secret confirmation I was looking for. God is good!!!! I, too, have restrained my feelings for a while, not exactly sure of when I should say what, but I do feel I am in love with you. I feel a deep connection between us, Jim.
>
> I have been praying for this moment in time for a long time. You were the special request I prayed for this past weekend; I asked God for confirmation about my feelings towards you, and He provided it, and without sounding like an unbeliever, I asked for a second confirmation and you provided that. I am so happy. This is about all I can get out now because I'm so happy, sorta speechless, sorta awestruck, but very happy.
>
> Sorry this is so short, but you've left me speechless. Thank you for being bold enough to share your inner most feelings with me.

The calm became excitement again! As soon as he finished reading the message, he went back to the start and read it all over again. He tried to recall Maria's voice and imagine what it would sound like if she were reading it to him aloud in her Texas accent. He pictured her smiling sweetly as she did so. He just wanted to give her a big hug right there and then. Each time he read it, there was something different he hadn't picked up on before. His face was flushed, and his hands were still shaking. Tears were starting to form; songs were coming to mind! Who could he tell first? So many emotions all replacing each other in turn, happiness like he'd never experienced before.

The more he reflected on things, the more he saw how every situation in which he found himself along the way had been divinely pieced together in bringing him to where he was now. It was as if the curtains were pulled back and every single thing that had happened since he first set foot in San Antonio nine months ago was staring him in the face with an explanation from God next to each one.

What if Martin had come with me the very first time like he was supposed to? What if I chose to stop that cab instead of having that cigarette? What if I'd been able to speak to Maria the first time I had the chance? What if I hadn't ended up in hospital that time? What if my blood tests hadn't gone missing? What if I had decided to have a drink in New Orleans and not go to San Antonio? What if Violet didn't have to go out of town that weekend? What if I had given that girl on the plane my phone number? What if I hadn't been able to get those two extra days off to go with Darius? What if…

He gasped as he realized what an awesome God he served! There was no other reason for the way things happened the way they did—he knew God had to have orchestrated the whole thing! And to think that God Almighty was responsible for bringing him such joy and for bringing such a unique and special lady into his life the way He did was more than he could comprehend. He began to weep some more. His faith had just been taken to a whole new level, and now he felt like it was strong enough to believe for absolutely anything, and since he still lived in the UK, and Maria was in Texas, he was going to have to put his faith into practice all over again. If he were to be with her on a full-time basis, he was going to have to believe for an even bigger miracle.

The journey was just beginning.

Chapter Six

With each day that followed their confession, Jim's and Maria's love for one another began to grow. On one side, Maria's background and personal status meant she had a more guarded approach to steering herself within the relationship, and thus she proceeded slowly. On the other, Jim had his foot on the gas pedal of his emotions, which he frequently and openly shared in the e-mails that connected him to her for the next three months.

Similarly their love for God was also increasing. Not one e-mail went by without recognition of God's role in bringing them together or His handling of their current situation. Talk about the future was limited, and usually only went as far as the next time they would see each other or of immigration options, but there did exist an unspoken appreciation of the fact that God was in control, which would later need to be called upon if things were to progress.

For the time being, the excitement of being in the new and obscure situation that was their relationship was refreshing.

Jim started by canceling existing plans he had to visit Australia the following year in favor of taking the time off near Christmas, instead, and returning to San Antonio for a sixth time. His joyful attitude at work continued to draw attention to himself, and he was only too willing to share his reasons for it whenever anyone asked. He was advised on more than one occasion by passengers (one of whom a talent scout) that he should go into show business on account of his comedic delivery of the onboard announcements, which had now received an injection of new life.

Maria loved having someone with whom she could talk about her day, share her feelings, and unburden her concerns. Her relationship with her family improved. Even her choir director remarked to her that her usual smile was brighter than ever.

They both sent gifts and cards by mail. Each others' accents were still novel to listen to, and voice mails were kept and replayed for days. Maria became more proficient in sending text messages, of which previously she'd had little experience or need. Jim became more proficient in talking slower on the phone in his Scottish accent on the few occasions he'd call her.

The pinnacle of it all for Jim came in an e-mail from Maria less than two weeks after she'd first said, "I love you." In response to him sharing some self-deprecatory thoughts he'd been entertaining that day about her wanting to be with him, Maria wrote:

> I trust you, Jim. Just wanted you to know that.

To Jim, "I trust you" seemed greater than "I love you." He always had a nagging doubt that beneath everything, Maria might be harboring some skepticism of his motives. He had no basis on which to form such an idea other than the countless stories he'd heard of foreign visitors preying on susceptible natives in order to gain access into a country. He wondered if Maria had heard similar stories. Hearing her now voice her trust in him, however, was quite possibly the best thing she'd ever written.

As for Maria, she was simply enjoying the way in which she could talk about all things pertaining to her faith in Jesus with someone who was of a similar knowledge and who was equally enthusiastic. She'd previously vowed that if she was ever to become involved with a man again that he would have to be a Christian first and foremost. Now that it was happening, she was realizing how important it had been to wait, and how, in the past, the imbalance of not being with such a man had adversely affected her in her previous relationships. Her time spent at church was now more meaningful, her desire to learn increased considerably, and her praise and worship was even more vibrant. This could be especially detected in the e-mails she'd send on a Sunday, which Jim often described as "buzzin'!"

Communicating by e-mail had several advantages. It seemingly allowed the pair to share more personal information than they would under the usual protocol of a dating couple who were not separated by distance. The need to make a message interesting to its reader meant a greater inclusion of self-detail, in addition to how the day had gone, in order to fill it up. Another bonus was that one could write something and then delete it again after consideration prior to sending. And being unable to see facial reactions to the information disclosed was also beneficial when it came to the more serious or embarrassing issues. Nevertheless, now that trust had been established, such issues were of smaller concern.

In spite of this, e-mailing was soon an inadequate substitute for being together in person, and the three months Jim and Maria were apart started to feel a whole lot longer. Maria began having problems with work, her health, and family matters. Jim, too, was being overloaded with work. He was also having to deal with a further loss of two close friends in quick succession. Just a couple of days spent together somewhere in the middle of it all seemed to be the perfect antidote to all the depression, but this time there would be insufficient finances and no available scope for shift-tinkering. On top of it all, continued research into immigration options brought more despondency, as the rules threw up yet more restrictions of which they were previously unaware.

Jim sought solace in the Lord. He felt reminded of the verse in the Bible that states, "Be still, and know that I am God" (Psalm 46:10). He also read, "So let us seize and hold fast and retain without wavering the hope we cherish and confess and our acknowledgement of it, for He who promised is reliable and faithful to His Word" (Hebrews 10:23, Amplified). And in a telephone conversation with Darius around the same time, Darius reminded him again to take things "little by little."

"Okay," Jim prayed to God. "If You're really telling me to do nothing for now, Lord, so be it! I'll do what You say. You know my track record when it comes to having patience though."

He continued to shower Maria with adoration and loving words, but to the point where she became unsettled, unused to being the focus of such overwhelming attention. He didn't seem to be doing anything wrong; just the "transition from not having someone to having someone," as she put it, was proving difficult to handle and, moreover, incorporate into her increasingly busy schedule. Her heart, which had become fortified from years of being single and a parent, was starting to feel fragile again, and the strengthening exercises of the past eight years would now have to be let go.

She continued to e-mail but to a lesser extent as time went by. Personal details gave way to lengthier descriptions of how the day had been or how the basketball was going. The "I love you" sign-off was substituted for a less-convincing "Love ya" or none at all.

Although no physical contact had yet taken place between the pair, Jim longed to give Maria a hug and assure her that everything would eventually work itself out. He explained how he'd heard from God, but it appeared that the words in the e-mails were having less impact, as evidenced by her wavering responses. Once again, doubts as to her willingness to keep going with him were starting to take up residence inside him, and on both sides, their responses to other people's questions on how things were going were waning in their enthusiasm.

He continued to cling to God's instructions to "be still" and the hope that he and Maria would eventually be together on account of Darius's prophecy. As a way to take his mind off things, he embarked upon a three-day trip to the Highlands of his native Scotland to spend time alone with God amid the lochs and mountains. During his trip he felt he heard God warning him of a *specific* battle ahead, supported by a dream he was to have of himself in the front line of the Scottish army resembling a scene from the film *Braveheart*. In this dream, however, instead of standing beside the leader, William Wallace, it was as if he stood alongside Jesus Who was encouraging him, saying he was not to be afraid of the enemy; he was "ready!" and He (Jesus) would be right there with him the whole time.

Two days later, on his way home from the Highlands, he was unable to obtain a staff ticket for the plane until two hours before it was due to leave. The plane was full, and he nervously ran the risk of being unable to travel and having to make a thirteen-hour bus journey instead. In the end, one seat did become available, and he was able to fly home after all—but it was close! He gave God the glory for seeing to it that he got that seat, but he wasn't convinced that this was the battle to which his dream referred. That was still to come, he sensed.

Maria, too, sought God for help. She asked for a return to the way she'd been feeling a short while back when her faith levels were high and her happiness was at its peak. Not long afterwards a friend, who was unaware of the way she'd been feeling, came to her and said, "I've got a word for you from the Lord: 'Don't give up'!"

At church the following week, the message from the pulpit was entitled "Enduring the Storm," from which she was able to draw much encouragement and personal application. In that same service, she closed her eyes and had a vision of Jim standing alongside with his arm around her as they worshiped together. Jim had shared an almost-identical vision with her that he'd had the week before. On a separate occasion, another friend came to her with a word of encouragement, saying, "This too shall pass." She knew as well that Jim was always praying for her.

All these things indeed brought much revival to her feelings for short periods of time but were swallowed up again amid the rigors of everyday life, amongst which she continued to wonder if she'd be able to keep a long-distance relationship going. She knew she loved Jim, and she wanted to be with him, but the uncertainty of how things would ever progress was keeping her in check. She cut back on the e-mailing and decided to wait until the next time she saw him again, which was fast approaching, to see what this time would bring.

Chapter Seven

At last it had arrived, the return to San Antonio! To Jim the only other time three months ever felt as long as these last three had was as a child knowing in advance he would be getting a Millennium Falcon for Christmas! This time round, just to see Maria's smile again seemed like it would bring more joy than even a real Millennium Falcon would ever have brought him!

The trip had been booked well in advance, in February of that year, before Jim and Maria had been introduced. There would be six traveling: Jim; his mother, Ruth; his grandmother, Granny; his brother Martin; his sister Stacey; and her friend, Samantha. They had listened to Jim's stories and watched the DVDs of the festival he'd been to the previous year and were keen to sample it for themselves this time round.

Financial considerations at the time meant the trip was only booked from the Thursday to the following Tuesday—only four whole days if traveling days were excluded and three of which would be taken up attending the festival. Now with a little more money available, it seemed a shame to not spend more time there.

Restrictions on the tickets, however, meant that changes were not permitted. The airline was unsympathetic to their pleas for an extension, and to purchase six new tickets would be too costly. Jim tried all he could think of, including making use of his contacts within the airline industry, to come up with something that would allow the family to stay longer but to no avail. The added frustration of only being able to spend such a limited time with Maria made it all the more difficult to take.

And so he prayed, "Lord, I know it's a big ask, but with You nothing is impossible. It would be so good if we were able to spend even a couple more days in San Antonio, and if You could arrange for that to happen, we'd be so grateful…"

The day before departure, he went online to check the status of the flights (normally he wouldn't do this, but for some reason this time he felt compelled to.) There were changes to the itinerary that the airline had made without informing them. Instead of everyone returning as a group on Tuesday as planned, five of them were now returning on a much earlier flight that day, and, worse still, Samantha had been changed to travel on her own on Monday.

To accept the changes without query was impossible: Samantha had learning difficulties and was incapable of flying from America to England on her own. Likewise for Martin. Stacey had Down's Syndrome, and Granny had difficulty traveling between her age and health concerns. That meant that all four of them needed to be together with either Jim or Ruth as their guardian. Ruth, too, had health problems that restricted her physical capabilities. Thus, if anyone were to be traveling home a day early on his or her own, it would need to be Jim. *No airline in the world is going to limit time spent with Maria, no way!* he swore. Unfortunately he was due at work for an eleven-hour shift that day.

He managed to get hold of his mother at her work right before his shift was due to start. He explained the predicament, told her where she could obtain the airline's phone number, and left her to deal with it. As he turned his phone off, he began praying some more. Any chance he got that day he prayed, and so it continued throughout the next ten hours onboard the airplane he was consigned to. If the last three months felt like the longest in history, these final ten hours were true to form in a similar fashion!

Finally the day at work ended. He turned his phone back on to see if there were any messages. There weren't. His mother was due to pick him up from work to take him back to her house where he'd spend the few hours before leaving for the airport by bus early in the morning (a different airport to the one from which he worked). He couldn't wait that long until she arrived—he called her.

"I'll tell you what they said when I get there to pick you up," she said, solemnly.

"No, just tell me now!"

"I can't, I'm driving!"

"Just *tell me*!"

"I'll be there in five minutes!" And with that, she hung up.

Ruth pulled up in the car to where Jim was standing waiting. Her face did not seem to imply she had good news. Jim got in and she drove off again.

"Well?" Jim asked, almost exploding with impatience at the silence that greeted him.

"How does two extra days sound?"

It took a few moments for Jim to forgive his mother of the cruel way in which she'd tantalized him concerning the outcome of the flights, but it wasn't long before he was beaming his delight at her efforts. Since the fault for the disruption lay with the airline, Ruth was able to secure seats for them all to come back on a flight two days later than originally planned, and Jim's prayers had been answered. Once again he offered up his familiar prayer of thanks: "*Thank You. Thank You. Thank You. Thank You. Thank You*!"

It was only four hours before he would need to be getting ready to leave for the airport to catch the flights to San Antonio, and despite feeling completely drained and exhausted, sleep was denied him as his brain continually reflected on the goodness of God in making the seemingly impossible, possible. *Awesome! Just… awesome!*

Chapter Eight

Two flights and many hours later, the family arrived in San Antonio and were met by Steve and Diane, who were happy to provide transportation for the group during their visit. Jim and Martin were staying at their house again, while Ruth, Granny, Stacey, and Samantha were residing in a nearby hotel. By the time everyone was settled into their lodgings, it was late at night, so Jim left contacting Maria until the following morning, whereupon he sent her a text and later spoke on the phone. She was working, so it would be evening before they would get to see each other again.

Just being in the same city as the love-of-his-life was a great feeling in itself. Accompanying said feeling, however, were notions of self-doubt as he entertained a concept that somehow Maria might be disappointed once she was with him again in person. Countless rejections in the past in other relationships had left him vulnerable in that respect. Hiding behind a computer screen or a telephone had become quite comfortable, but now he was to be fully exposed when they'd meet up, and he suddenly didn't mind if the long wait to finally be together again became longer—enough time until he could find some confidence in himself again. It didn't help knowing that his family would probably be analyzing his every effort, too.

Unknown to Jim, Maria was having similar feelings. Jim composed good e-mails, and she loved the words he wrote and spoke to her, but would she love the real thing just as much? How would he act should they end up alone together? How would *she* act should they end up alone together, come to think of it? The distance barrier was now removed, and the nerves had filled its place. She, too, felt that the scrutiny of her friends and family would be upon her, and being the center of attention was not something she enjoyed in a small setting.

Consequently, at the festival, the anticipated super-charged emotion of the reunion was quenched amid feelings of awkwardness and nerves. Jim entered the church behind his family via the side door next to the stage where Maria had already taken her place among the choir and was about to begin rehearsing for the service. She spotted their entry and smiled in turn as each member of his family recognized her and waved. As Jim brought up the rear and she saw him, she blushed, as suddenly the anxiety and feelings of being watched became apparent.

Jim silently gestured with his hand for her to take note of where they were sitting and to come and join them once she'd finished singing; however, her son Isaac had already kept her a place on the other side of the auditorium, which she was unable to convey in reply. As such, the reunion was delayed further until after the service had finished.

Immediately following the service was a fireworks display to officially mark the commencement of the festival. The fairground rides were already in full-swing, and the booths were selling all different types of food. Finally it happened: they met. A brief embrace was followed by the individual introductions of Maria to the family. She had heard lots about them through Jim's e-mails and so felt familiar enough to offer each of them a hug. As Martin stepped out from his, he looked at Jim and said, "She's *wonderful*!"

Jim's sister Stacey was very impressed too. "Maria is perfect—she is the one for you!" she told Jim excitedly. An element of Stacey's condition meant that her emotions were honest and strong in the extreme. For her to consent to someone potentially removing her big brother from her life was a huge endorsement as far as Jim was concerned. Ordinarily if she didn't like someone, she'd be sure to let them know!

Ruth, Granny, and Samantha also voiced their approval.

Despite countless hours of conversations by e-mail, Jim found himself struggling for something to say now she was in front of him. It wasn't the lack of topics holding him back, just the fear of saying something stupid on their first night together officially as a couple. In fact, Jim's mother spent more time talking with her than he did, and she was feeling ill—a negative reaction to painkillers she'd taken the day before—although she hid it well underneath the excitement of meeting this wonderful lady she'd heard so much about.

Ruth's illness, together with the effects of jetlag that everyone was feeling, meant the time spent together was altogether limited. Since Jim was at the mercy of Steve and Diane for a ride home along with the family, he had to respect their wishes to leave even though he would've loved to have stayed longer. As they parted company, Maria went back to enjoying the festivities for a while, and Jim trudged off to his ride. The first day together had ended with just as many questions with which it had started and disappointingly offered little indication of what the future held.

The next day was to be much better. The whole family, along with Steve and Diane, met with Maria and Isaac for lunch at a restaurant. Isaac's cousin of the same age, Arnold, also came along. Jim sat next to Maria at the table with Ruth and Stacey directly across from them.

Ruth was a bubbly character who simply loved to talk and meet new people, so Jim was content to sit back and let her chat with Maria while he mentally took notes of their conversations. It was clear she'd all but overcome the sickness that had dogged her the previous day as she joyfully set about getting to know her new friend.

Stacey, too, was enjoying the occasion. She'd been warned in advance not to ask Maria any deep or personal questions, as she was inclined to do, but it didn't stop her from wanting to pose for as many photographs with her brother's new woman as she could. Ones of her in the middle of the couple were even better as far as she was concerned.

As Stacey positioned herself between Jim and Maria for a snapshot, Jim found himself closer to Maria than he'd ever been before. It was then he really began to notice just how physically attractive she actually was. She was wearing a white t-shirt that contrasted against her smooth, dark skin, making it all the more noticeable, and pink lipstick that highlighted the perfect shape of her lips. Her long brown hair reached the small of her back—something else that had previously gone unnoticed—and her long eyelashes fully exposed her gorgeous brown eyes. In the past it had primarily been her faith and disposition with which he was so enthralled, but now her outward appearance had fully gotten his attention. No doubt about it—she was beautiful!

The clicking of the camera being pointed in their direction brought him back to reality, and he quickly re-adjusted his focus on the side of Maria he already knew, her character. Underneath it all he still secretly hoped Stacey would not get tired of taking photographs and posing in them so as he'd have a nice collection when he went home.

A few hours later, it was back to the church for the second night of the festival. After Maria had finished singing with the choir, she made her way back to the row of seats in which the family was sitting adjacent to Isaac and his cousin Arnold. As she headed towards Jim, Isaac purposefully shuffled along to leave a space for her in between himself and Granny, who sat beside him, leaving Jim further down the row next to Arnold. Maria reluctantly accepted Isaac's determination of the seating arrangements, and since he had no choice, so did Jim.

Their thoughts were soon to be diverted as the guest speaker began his sermon. Teaching from the Bible from the book of Acts, he urged, "Remember, midnight is the darkest part of the night… but it's also the closest minute to the day!"

Both Jim and Maria were alerted by his words. Not knowing what each other was thinking certainly felt like being in the dark and what seemed like the midnight of being separated again by distance was already too close for comfort. *Could there actually be day to follow it?*

The preacher continued, "Whenever the devil comes at you with venom and great oppression like never before, you know that you are closer than ever to a huge breakthrough in your life!"

These were more heartening words to which they could appropriate their situation. All the negativity that had engulfed their minds of late seemed to be intensifying, and the cloudiness surrounding the future would not leave them alone. To know that all this aggravation was just a prelude to a major triumph ahead would all be worthwhile if it proved true.

"Fear not—God will not only bring you through the trouble," he summarized, "God will bring you *through* the trouble!"

With the help of hand gestures to illustrate his point, he conveyed a forceful charge as opposed to simply being escorted. It implied a dramatic victory over circumstances versus a laborious trudge.

Such imagery and rousing speech provoked a response in Jim that ultimately made him glad he wasn't sitting next to Maria at this point! He erupted in praise and worship to God with shouts and tears as if he were the only one in the room (fortunately most of the congregation, including Maria, was doing the same) as Arnold watched on in bewilderment. The message he'd just heard was as if it had been spoken directly to him by God Himself, promising him that an end to all the uncertainty was on its way, and nothing could hold him back in his gratitude!

The happiness carried on into the night as everyone headed outside to watch another superb fireworks display. Stacey set about obtaining more photographs, and Granny showed she was not too old to party as she danced along with the live band that was playing. Jim felt at ease as he sat beside Maria and engaged her in more relaxed and meaningful conversations than he'd managed in the past. *If ever a night was not meant to end, this was it!* he thought.

Alas, the night did end, but it was it was only ten hours before he was back at church attending the early Sunday morning service. Sleep had been difficult to come by during the night, but being in the six thousand-seat auditorium again with so many fellow believers and being able to watch Maria shining on stage as she sang was sufficient enough to energize him to almost the same extent as he was the night before. He took a seat next to Isaac and watched as the choir sung,

> I must tell Jesus;
> I must tell Jesus;
> Oh I cannot bear these burdens alone.
> I must tell Jesus;
> I must tell Jesus;
> Jesus can help me, Jesus alone.

Maria came and sat next to Isaac and Jim after she'd finished singing. For all they were in church and listening intently to what was being spoken from the pulpit, it still felt nice to finally be attending a service together.

Immediately following the service, she hugged Jim and left to go and sell refreshments, which she did every week on behalf of the single-family ministry of the church to which she belonged. A minute later, she came running back and grabbed Jim by the hand.

"Come with me, there's someone I want you to meet," she said.

"Aye, okay," Jim replied eagerly.

Maria introduced him to her friend and Bible study group leader, John, whom she also described as being like her "spiritual father." John was from India, yet he'd lived in San Antonio for many years and so was adept at understanding American English. But as Jim opened his mouth and spoke his Scottish version of the English language, it was clear it was being received with difficulty. Nevertheless, the meeting was a success, and as Jim left Maria, he couldn't help but wonder what the significance of it all was. Maria's own father had died five years ago, so to be acquainted with her spiritual father felt like just as important an introduction in the whole scheme of things. He walked away smiling, unaware that behind him, John was giving his initial approval of him to Maria.

Later that day Maria returned from her home to pick up Jim from church where he had been enjoying the festival with his family since the church services had finished earlier in the day. Isaac and Arnold were playing a basketball game for their local team, and even though basketball was not his favorite sport, it was still an opportunity for him to spend more time with Maria. When they arrived at the game, he was introduced to Maria's sister Carmen and her husband, Dan, who were already sitting in the bleachers and looking forward to meeting him.

Jim used to his advantage his knowledge of previous events in their family history of which Maria had supplied details in her e-mails and soon felt as if he had been accepted by them, too, as a welcome addition in their sister's life. Following the game he went back to church where he met more of Maria's friends before she had to leave to take her place in the choir for the evening service. Once again the fact that he was being presented to so many different people in Maria's life gave him confidence he was going to feature in it beyond his stay in San Antonio. Yet still he could not help wondering in what capacity. Moreover, he couldn't help wondering if he would actually get the chance to spend time with her alone, just the two of them, to find out for sure just how compatible they were in each other's company without computer screens or friends in between them. That had been penciled in for the following day, which Maria had taken off work, but with all the distractions of family and other matters, there was always a risk it wasn't going to happen.

After the evening event, she came over and spent a little time with Jim's family before leaving with Isaac for home. She confirmed to him she was all-clear to meet with him the next day. At home, as she lay down in bed, it took her a long while before she was able to fall asleep, anxious of how the next day was going to turn out. Similarly Jim was spending his time awake praying to God that tomorrow would at long last give a clearer indication of their future together.

Finally, they had their first real date as a couple after nearly five months of being together!

Chapter Nine

Maria arrived early to pick up Jim from Steve and Diane's house. Steve was up and about and jokingly instructed them to "behave themselves" before allowing them to take off together.

"Y'all be good now!" he shouted as they climbed into the car.

As they pulled away in the car, Maria asked Jim if he was okay about meeting with her mother and going for breakfast with her. *Another step in the right direction,* he thought, even though it would cut into the time he'd hoped they would be spending alone with each other.

Maria's mother, Alice, ordinarily was shy when it came to being with someone she'd never met before—it was just part of her nature. Unaware of this, Jim interpreted her quietness as being her way of sounding him out, and his initial reaction was that she was quite imposing. He made sure he conducted himself with chivalry of the highest standards and kept his nicotine gum (upon which he was still heavily dependent) out of sight.

In reality nothing could have been further from the truth. Alice was suitably impressed with his behavior and soon the conversation began flowing in a more relaxed manner as the three enjoyed breakfast at a nearby diner. Until he became "poisoned."

Jim was allergic to caffeine. It caused in him an inability to breathe regularly, an impairment of his vision, and pains in his chest. Whenever he ordered coffee, he would always overstress the importance to the vendor that it was decaffeinated to ensure they wouldn't accidentally serve him regular. On this occasion, however, he neglected to do so and soon he realized that what he'd been drinking was not what he'd asked for.

The reaction usually kicked in relatively slowly, so it wasn't until they got up to leave that it began to take effect. He began clawing at himself and covering his mouth with his hand as he tried to minimize his distress, hoping it would somehow subside or maybe even calm down for a moment, at least long enough until Alice was no longer with them so as not to make a scene in front of her.

Thankfully he did manage to contain himself long enough until they'd dropped Alice back at her home and were on the road again when he was at last able to confess to Maria that he was in trouble.

"I just need a big bottle of water so that I can flush it out of my system," he explained.

"Well we can't stop here—this is a bad neighborhood."

"I don't care—I grew up in bad neighborhoods! I'll take my chances!" Jim retorted sharply. "Just stop the car at the nearest store! I'll go in and buy it. I'm not bothered!"

Maria appeared shocked at this forceful side of Jim she'd never encountered before and eventually pulled the car into a gas station. As she went in a bought a large bottle of water for him, Jim stayed in the car uttering panic-stricken prayers to God that he'd be able to overcome the allergic reaction and continue the date.

"Here you go," Maria said as she handed him the water upon her return to the car.

"Thanks!"

They pulled away in silence, and Jim slaked almost the whole bottle in one go. Soon he gradually began to recover, and as he reflected on the situation that had gone before, he realized his abruptness in dealing with Maria and his request for aid.

Great start! he thought.

He apologized to Maria, and soon the date was back on. In the course of the next hour, he progressed back to normal health as he and Maria went to a couple of stores in search of gifts she wanted to buy for his family as mementos of their stay in America. The conversation was light, and the time spent was enjoyable. It would seem a shame to threaten it with a heavy discussion about the future.

"Where to next?" Maria asked after they'd finished buying gifts.

"I dunno. How about the zoo?"

"The zoo?"

"Aye, zoos are great fun! You can get a good laugh at the animals doing stuff sometimes!"

"Uh . . . okay."

It took longer than expected to reach the zoo, so by the time they got there, the cost of entering it was not worth the expense based on the available time they had left together. Maria had to leave within a couple of hours to pick up Isaac from school, and she first had to drop Jim off. Outside the zoo, however, was a beautiful park in which they were able to go for a walk. As Jim continued to keep his hands to himself, Maria concluded that his gentlemanly nature was not just a pretense and he truly was the honorable person he portrayed himself to be. She'd previously never doubted his virtue, yet strangely she'd been nervous about actually being alone with him, perhaps as a result of past encounters or stories she'd heard of others' experiences, she wasn't sure. Now the remainder of her inhibitions were subsiding and confidence was taking over.

She pointed out the various plants and trees, naming each one as they walked and giggled like a schoolgirl as she collected a handful of pecans from the ground and playfully bounced them off Jim at close range. And after a ride on the miniature train, she suggested they sit on a bench together and just talk for a while.

This was what Jim was waiting for, the chance to talk. The chance to find out her view on things and how she regarded their situation. He was already confident that, even though it was still going to take a miracle, they would ultimately end up together—God had already told him that, and he just wondered if He'd told her yet. By no means was he going to bring up the possibility of them ever being married to each other, but he was going to have to find another way of discussing their potential without mentioning it.

The conversation was getting deeper. There were things Maria was able to share about her past, which previously she'd deliberately omitted from e-mails in case they'd be too in-depth or misread. Similarly Jim shared with her the truth about incidents in his life from which he'd previously held back from everyone else. Yet for some strange reason, he was unable to force the questions to which he so desperately needed answers past his lips. In a similar situation to the night he first stood next to her a year ago, he opened his mouth to speak but the words would not come out. *Not again!* he groaned.

As they got up to leave and headed back to the car, he persisted in his efforts to engage Maria in matters of the heart, yet each time was silenced by an inward force that would not permit him. The conversation was still flowing between them all the way back to Steve and Diane's house, but nothing that would enlighten either of them as to where their future lay.

"I'll see you tomorrow then?" Jim asked Maria when they reached the house.

"Sure!" Maria replied emphatically.

I'll try again tomorrow! he reassured himself as he got out of the car. He waved to Maria as she drove off, sighed, then slowly made his way inside.

"*Well?*" his mother Ruth asked him as soon as he opened the door.

"'Well' what?"

"What happened?" she inquired, impatiently.

"Well, we went for breakfast this morning with her Ma, then we went to a couple of shops. Then we went to a park and went on a wee train and–"

"Never mind that, did you sort out where you're going from here?"

"Nah."

"What do you mean, 'Nah'? That was the whole point of going out was it not?"

"Never got the chance," Jim replied, his irritation starting to rise within.

"But you had all day..."

"*I know!*" he finally snapped, making it clear that he was just as disappointed with the outcome as everyone else in the room who was expecting to hear some news.

"Oh!" Ruth murmured softly, bringing an end to that part of the conversation. "Well we had a *lovely* day!" she went on cheerfully, trying to lift the mood back to the way it was before he came in.

Feeling guilty himself, he tried to restore his own temperament to appear excited for the rest of them who'd spent the day in downtown San Antonio for the first time, but really all he wanted to do was head to his room and reflect on what went wrong. His misery was further compounded when Maria sent him a text saying that the plans they'd made to meet with John, her Bible Study group leader, the next night would have to be canceled on account that he now couldn't make it. Instead, she agreed to come to dinner, which Diane had decided to cook for them, but it was doubtful they'd get another chance to talk since the whole family would be in attendance as well. The night after that, Maria would have choir practice, and the next day was when he was leaving for the UK. His chance, it seemed, had gone, and so it would be back to e-mailing again when he got home. The great day they'd spent together was soon forgotten about and replaced by the same perpetual negative thought patterns and prayers that had kept him occupied in the past: "What's going on Lord? What's going on?" he pleaded with God.

Unfortunately for Jim, God was keeping silent. There were only two days left of the vacation with little scope for any more progress, and the breakthrough he felt was coming when he rejoiced so vehemently at church a few days ago now seemed like an impossibility.

To make matters worse, Maria called and said she would be unable to come for dinner on the grounds that she had to go to the stores with Isaac to buy him a jacket for school. At that, the voices of discontent inside Jim's head began singing loudly, "*Got to buy Isaac a jacket for school"? Here you are, five thousand miles from home, only here for two more days, supposedly in love, and she wants to go shopping instead of meeting you? What's that all about? Why would she want to do that tonight when she can do it every other day of the year when you're not here? Sounds like an I-want-out excuse to me!*

To listen to those voices was easy; to rebuke them, not so. The unfounded thought that Maria wanted to end her part in the relationship took root almost immediately, and Jim felt physically ill. The only rational argument to counter it was the fact that he'd been introduced to so many people in her life over the course of his stay—especially John—which she wouldn't have otherwise done if she'd planned on ending things, but then maybe that was just her being polite. *And did John cancel that evening, or was she just saying that?*

He began to dissect the date they'd been on, analyzing everything he'd said and done on it and looking for some hint or clue of something that could've changed her mind about him. The only thing, he figured, that could've made the date responsible for a change in heart was the fact they hadn't discussed where they were going. *Surely that couldn't be it?*

In any case, he knew and trusted Maria well enough to know that she was not one to hold back from sharing her feelings, however bad or good they were. *Maybe she was just waiting until I left to break the news so as not to spoil the rest of my vacation!*

In addition, he was having to field questions from everyone as to whether he and Maria were still going strong and why she was not being able to make it to dinner. He bluffed an assurance that everything was fine and that the reason she would not be there was because she had something on to do with Isaac's school that night that she'd forgotten about. He decided to leave out the part about her buying a jacket for Isaac, since it would no doubt give rise to the same questions he was already asking himself. Right there and then, though, and just as he spoke those words, it instantly hit home the responsibility she had to Isaac as his mother and that it was always going to be of the highest priority, more so than her responsibility to him ever would be. With that in mind, he knew he would have to be noble and stand aside and respect her decision to uphold her commitment to Isaac, no matter how strongly he felt about a future she might have with him. Still he couldn't help thinking, *Could this be a reason for things to end?*

Ultimately he reflected on the distinct lack of "I love you's" there seemed to have been since he'd arrived in San Antonio. The passion and excitement that had been declared three months ago by e-mail had been noticeably weaker the closer it got to his visit and seemingly absent since he got there. *Had the love really disappeared or are we both just too afraid to mention it?*

The negativity consuming him was starting to manifest itself in more ways than one. He was unable to finish his dinner that evening, and the following day he was even more quiet and withdrawn as he went with Steve and the rest of his family on a trip to the Texas Hill Country. Each time he thought of Maria breaking up with him, he began to shake and would have to clench his teeth to stifle the sick feeling arising from within.

All he could do was cling desperately to his recollection of the events at church at the weekend; to the words of the song:

> I must tell Jesus;
>
> I must tell Jesus;
>
> Oh I cannot bear these burdens alone…

…and the words of the preacher: "Whenever the devil comes at you with venom and great oppression like never before, you know that you are closer than ever to a huge breakthrough in your life!"

It was true. He'd never felt such an onslaught of defeatism in as far back as he could ever remember. He kept reminding himself that he had no evidence on which to base all his pessimistic conclusions, so where was all this coming from? Nothing else could rationally explain it—surely there *must* be a breakthrough on the way!

At 6:33 p.m. his phone announced a text message had come through. It was from Maria and it read, "I'll be able to come over after practice for a little while if that's okay?"

His spirits were instantly lifted, as were those of his family who were with him at the house. They were anxious to know what was happening and whether they would get to see Maria again before they left.

Regardless of what was going to happen in the short time Maria was over, Jim was determined he was going to be happy. When she arrived two hours later, he answered the door and gleefully announced her arrival to everyone as she entered.

She brought two bags filled with the gifts she'd bought for the family on her day out with him two days previously. In the middle of distributing them, she discreetly handed Jim a letter, which he took and placed under his leg as he sat. Thinking it could possibly contain the last words she'd ever write him, he decided to avoid reading it until after she left, all the while still managing to keep up his happy charade.

Maria stayed for around an hour, posing for more photos for Stacey and enduring lively conversations with Ruth and Granny who had really taken a shine to Maria in the limited time they'd had together. Finally it came time for her to leave, and as everyone got in line to say their respective final farewells by the front door, Jim hung back and quickly opened his letter, his impatience eventually getting the better of him. He knew he didn't have enough time to read it all, he just wanted to see how it ended. And as he read, tears filled his eyes. In closing she wrote, "Look forward to more fun times in the future. Love you, Maria."

Wherever she'd been the last couple of days and whatever had been going on in her life that had caused her to be distant didn't matter now! All he knew was that their relationship was still on and would continue to be so even after he left.

As he read the last two lines over again, it dawned on him that she would probably be nearing the end of her goodbyes and waiting for him to have his turn. He took a deep breath, wiped his eyes, and hurried back towards the front door, which was now open with her standing in it and just about to leave. She smiled as she saw him reenter the room. In his absence she considered that maybe he found farewells too hard to handle and had deliberately refrained from taking part. But now, at the back of the crowd, there he was, ready to escort her out.

The door closed behind them as they walked towards her car. She reached out to open the door, but Jim put his hand on her arm and gently turned her around. He looked into her eyes, and for the first time face to face he said, "I love you."

Maria smiled back and said, "I love you too."

He reached out his arms and fully took hold of her. Breathing in the soft aroma of her hair, he felt her hands move slowly up and down his back as she shared in the embrace. He no longer felt the oppression that had persecuted him so violently. Instead it felt like a weight was being lifted and was being replaced by a sense of peace and renewed hope that everything was going to turn out okay. In that one hug, he realized he was going to spend the rest of his life with this woman whom he knew he already loved with all his heart.

"Thank you. I really needed to hear that," he whispered softly.

As they separated they looked again into each other's eyes and smiled. Words were no longer needed; everything they needed to say had already just been said in that one moment of contact. Everything except "goodbye."

Jim reached out his hand and opened the car door; Maria got in and looking out of the side window, waved to him as she drove off. She held back her tears until she was out of sight.

Walking back to the house, Jim, in a moment of appreciation of what had just taken place, remembered his God, looked to the sky, and whispered, "Thank You!"

Chapter Ten

Sitting on the plane leaving Texas, reading her letter for the tenth time, nothing, it seemed, could alter the peace he now felt nor wipe the smile off his face! Not even the plane breaking down and being forced to spend the night in a hotel in Detroit, or being sandwiched between two oversized bodies all the way back to the UK, or railway maintenance in London lengthening their journey home by another three hours.

In her letter Maria told of her joy in meeting Jim's family and the impact they'd had on her. She expressed her gratitude concerning his handling of her obligation to her son's needs, especially when their time together was so limited. And she revealed just how much she'd enjoyed those few precious hours they did spend together and how his gentlemanly behavior had impressed her.

She went on to say how much she was trusting God regarding the future. "The future is in His hands," she wrote. Over the next few days, she saw billboards outside of churches and heard radio programs all saying the same thing: "Trust God."

Trusting God was something she was becoming accustomed to of late. In the past she'd felt that she and Jim had been getting along too fast. She asked herself, *How can I be in love in such a little time? Is it really love?* The fact that she saw God involved in the instigation of their union, however, made it somehow different and thus easier to keep going. She e-mailed Jim,

> Having God involved in our relationship makes anything possible. Long relationship, short one, as long as God is in charge, it's all good. And getting involved with someone (again) was a little difficult at first. But I truly have felt a deep connection in our spirits, which gave me the all clear sign that it was okay/safe to let my heart out of its cage.

Another thing she couldn't get out her head was the fact that there had been no physical contact to date between her and Jim. This, of course, pleased her immensely since, as a Christian, she was compelled to live by the principles taught in the Bible. That Jim had not breached—nor even tried to breach—those principles spoke high volumes to her of his maturity in the faith as well as his character. Nevertheless, she also knew that there had been opportunities when, alone together, the chance to hold hands or even kiss had presented itself and natural curiosity of what it would have been like did cross her mind on more than one occasion. *That one hug on the last night together felt so good, too!* Ultimately, though, she recognized that this was not the defining element of their relationship and that their compatibilities at spiritual and emotional level would no doubt be just as effectual at physical level, too, were it permitted.

The more she reflected on all the things that had taken place since she'd first met him, the more she felt at ease and the more she allowed herself to consider the possibility that one day he might even become her husband. She knew Jim, she knew God, and she knew all things concerning their love were now clear in her head and in place were he ever to ask her.

What she didn't know was that Jim was closer to that moment than she realized. He basically had been since day one, so confident was he that God had predestined them to be together. Yet, aside from not wanting to rush things too fast, there was one other thing stopping him from mentioning marriage in any conversation or e-mail—the meal-ticket theory.

The meal-ticket theory had long been in his mind, even as far back as before he got to meet her. He thought that since she lived in America, and he'd previously expressed an interest in moving there, that people—especially on her side—would be suspicious that his motives for marrying her were for no other reason than to obtain residency in the United States. Those closest to him, including Maria, knew otherwise, yet still he saw scenarios play out in his head in which he'd be defending himself against people questioning their being together.

In the end, worrying about what other people thought took second place to his desire to be married to the lovely Maria. He had it in his mind that he would propose to her, ring and all, on his next visit to San Antonio, which was only five weeks away, but in her first e-mail to him after arriving back in the UK, she indirectly touched on the subject. She said,

> I have to back up and say that my good friend, Julie, said to me early on, when we were e-mailing each other, she asked me if I loved you. I told her yes and she said, "Well just tell him you love him, and he'll probably ask you to marry him"...Thanks Julie! Talk about pressure!!!

Without hesitation, Jim jumped on the defensive in his reply. He viewed Julie's comments as being stereotypical of those watching for a quick marriage proposal early on in their relationship with the meal-ticket theory at the back of their minds, even though in Julie's case, he guessed they probably weren't intended that way. Nevertheless it was a chance to now address it. He wrote:

> I'm conscious that you have many people in your life who (and I'm not saying they ever have or will but) could have made

believing in having a relationship with me a difficult thing for you. Like the marriage thing for example: Anyone could fill your head with thoughts that since I was keen to move to America then by hooking up with someone from the States could be an option for getting a visa. As I know you know, that concept doesn't even come into things when it comes to me.

Just so as you know, though, it is the main reason I've never asked you to marry me before. Or indeed, never brought up the m-word in any conversation or e-mail. As far as I can see from what's gone on up until this point, there is no reason why we aren't headed in that direction, but I'm trying to keep my feet on the ground and not move too far ahead of things. I don't know how you feel about it, but I can only assume for you to commit to that sort of level with someone again would be the ultimate act of bravery on your part. I really hope I haven't spoiled things by including all this stuff, but I just wanted to get it out into the open before any more time goes by. If it doesn't sit well with you, just put it down to the jetlag talking, and I won't bring it up again. I'm not asking you to marry me here—I'd never do that in an e-mail!—I just thought it might be good to talk about it, if only for just this once. You don't have to reply to it if you don't want to, though.

The palpitations Jim felt as he sent the message were likewise felt by Maria as she read it. Despite the assurances that he would never ask her to marry him in an e-mail, on both sides it seemed that that was exactly what had just happened. And Maria was as unlikely to refuse his caveat that she abstain from talking about it just as much as he was hoping she wouldn't.

Jim had to be at work at 5:15 a.m. the following morning. Normal practice was that he'd be in bed by 8 p.m. at the latest and be back up again seven hours later, but with all he'd just written in his e-mail, the ability to fall asleep had become more difficult. With jetlag still an issue, it was closer to impossible. Just as it was when he first declared his love to her, speculation as to what her reply might contain continued to fill his brain, and as a result, he was forced to spend the night watching the numbers change on his digital alarm clock.

At three thirty he got out of bed. He turned on his computer, but there was no reply from Maria, so he got ready for work then checked a second time. She still hadn't replied, so he headed to the airport. Upon arriving at the office he went onto the Internet and checked again. Still nothing. He conducted his usual pre-flight duties and briefed his crew, resigned to the notion that she wasn't going to reply. It was now 5:30 a.m.—11:30 p.m. in San Antonio—and it was more than likely she'd gone to bed by now.

Unusually however, the pilots for that day's duty were running late, and with five more minutes to spare, a voice inside Jim's head said, "Check again!" When he did, there was Maria's reply, and in it she said,

> You'll be glad to know, that NONE of my friends have even suggested to me that I could be your ticket to America. That's what I love about my friends. They are so genuine and loving. Bottom line: I won't worry (worrying doesn't help anyway) about what anybody thinks; it's just satan's way of trying to distort what God has created.

This in itself was enough to bring about a glut of emotion inside Jim, but nothing could prepare him for what she wrote next:

> I have a question for you. BRACE YOURSELF…I've been wanting to ask you how you feel about a family. I wanted to give you an opportunity to escape, if you think I am too old for you in the baby-making category…

At that moment the pilots for the day's duty came through announcing they were ready to leave to go to the airplane. His hand shaking like never before, Jim cleared the computer screen, and ,with a stunned look on his face, he turned to his crew and beamed, "I think I'm gonna get married!"

At 7:36 p.m. Jim called Maria.

"Hey Maria, how ye doin?"

"Good! You?"

"Aye, champion! I got your e-mail. Like, wow!"

Maria laughed. "What did you think?"

"About the 'baby-making' bit?" Jim asked, bluntly.

"Well, yeah. All of it really."

"Aye. Only thing is, if we were to have a baby, we'd need to be married first."

"Uh-huh."

"So ... erm ... will ye then? Marry me, I mean ...?"

So much for a perfect proposal! All the carefully-constructed prose he'd spent so long rehearsing had just been replaced by an unconvincing stammer. Nevertheless, Maria said, "Yes!"

Through her reply, Jim could almost see her smiling as she uttered her soft reply. Tears were starting to form in his eyes, and he imagined the same in hers. For a moment, he lost his ability to speak and had to cough just to let her know he was still there. Then when he regained a small decree of composure, he said, "Wow!"

It would probably take a while for the reality of what had just happened to sink in. Both their lives had changed forever, and for Jim, there was the added factor of having to uproot to America to consider. They spent the remaining minutes of the call discussing all the things they could think of that would need to take place, interspersed with more short periods of silence and utterances of "Wow!" In closing, Maria exclaimed, "God is good, isn't He?"

"Amen!" said Jim. "He sure is!"

Once they'd hung up, Jim went first into his sister's room where Stacey was sitting on her bed cutting up pictures from magazines for her scrapbook. He tiptoed up to her with a solemn look on his face and placed his forehead on hers, pretending as if he were about to say something serious, then whispered, "I'm getting married!"

A split-second later, Stacey's confusion became realization, and her puzzled look turned into one of sheer joy. She took a deep breath in, and as her eyes filled with tears, she put her arms round Jim's neck and hugged him tightly. When she let go she cried out, "*Muum*!"

By this time Ruth had made her way to her own room to read and watch TV from the comfort of her bed. She turned her head toward the open door to see Stacey charging down the hall, dragging Jim by the arm as she came.

"*My brother is getting married*!" Stacey declared with pride.

She looked up at Jim to confirm the report, and with a nod of his head and a smile, he validated Stacey's declaration. More tears and another round of hugs ensued, followed by a reaching for the phone in order to spread the word to as many friends as possible before it got too late at night.

As for Maria, she tried to go back to working again but was unable to concentrate. All she could think of was what everyone's reactions would be and, more importantly, who she was going to tell first. The decision was made for her that night when her daughter, Jacqueline, called. On hearing the news, Jacqueline immediately picked up her car keys and announced to her husband, "I'll be back—I'm going to Mom's!" She greeted Maria with shrill laughter and a hug. Even though she had yet to meet Jim, she knew the difference he'd made in her mother's life, so it was easy for her to give her approval. After she left, Maria called her two closest friends, who both were equally as pleased for her as Jacqueline had been.

The majority of the week that followed for both Maria and Jim was spent basking in the euphoria of being engaged and passing on the news to friends and families, being mindful to give God the glory for His part in it all. Jim joked that it was an arranged marriage—God arranged it! Just about everybody shared in their delight and wished them all the happiness and success they deserved; only Maria's son Isaac expressed disapproval.

Most of the congratulations were also accompanied by questions along the lines of "What happens next?" All Jim wanted was to be left alone, if only for a few days, to soak up the emotion of it all, but with the uncommon nature of their long-distance relationship, it was only natural that people would want to know how they were going to proceed. Over time he became disgruntled as a lot of the responses he received were more focused on how lucky he was to be moving to America rather than how blessed he was to be getting married. On Maria's side, the most common follow-up question was whether or not she'd be moving to the UK—something she told Jim she'd be willing to undertake if it was the only way she could be with him—but family commitments ultimately placed it at the bottom of the list of available options.

In both cases, however, nothing could take away the excitement of what the future held. With four more weeks to go until Jim's next trip, e-mails and telephone calls would once again have to make due, but they wouldn't make missing each other any easier. And four weeks now seemed a very, very long time!

Chapter Eleven

After about a week, Jim realized that he was not just getting married; he was getting married to the most beautiful woman he'd ever met, both inside and out, and she was perfectly suited for him too! She loved him as much as he loved her—something else that he'd never experienced before, even though he'd been engaged to be married in the past. That one was never going to work for so many reasons, least of all because the girl involved was not a Christian, and ultimately she did him a huge favor by ending things ahead of time. Now, here he was, involved with someone whom God had given him, and the contrast was sublime.

He reflected on his prayers in the past in which he'd asked God for a wife and the specific qualities she had to possess. First and foremost, she had to be a Christian, a devoted one at that. Another matter of huge importance was that she abstain from drinking. Having someone in his house under the influence of alcohol was not something he wanted to see no matter how rare an event it might be. She also had to have a good sense of humor, since humor was a big part of his own character: if she couldn't laugh on a regular basis, then she was no use! She had to be unselfish, kind, and caring. She had to like sports, singing, and movies. And she had to have a sense of adventure—*reserved, private,* or *boring* were not words that could ever be used to describe her.

Physically she had to be good-looking too. He didn't see this as a selfish request. He knew how important intimacy was in a marriage. If he were to be with someone he didn't find attractive, then he would not be sexually satisfied, and no matter how many of those other character qualities she had that he liked, if she weren't outwardly appealing to him, he knew it could still eventually cause problems.

Finally, in order to clinch the deal, she had to have an accent from anywhere but the UK. She didn't necessarily have to *live* outside the UK, just not speak with a British accent!

When he prayed for such a wife, he felt he'd stumped God. As time went by, and the longer he remained single, he thought about dropping a few items from the list or modifying it slightly. Now he had Maria, and recognizing how she was everything that he had prayed for in a wife, the verse in the Bible that states that "...with God, nothing will be impossible" was being proved right (Luke 1:37).

Maria also had her own list of attributes her future husband would need to have before she would ever consider being married again. Hers was nowhere near as long as Jim's, but it was, to a degree, as restrictive.

Most importantly, he had to be a Christian—there would be absolutely no deviating from that no matter how nice he was!

Secondly, he would have to come from within the church to which she was so devoted and value the words of its senior pastor as much as she did. Some weeks as she stood on the stage about to sing, she would scan the congregation, and for a moment, wonder where, if at all, her husband-to-be was standing. Little did she know, he was actually standing five thousand miles away, but one day would be in front of her by reason of a TV commercial!

He would have to be a non-smoker; smoking was something she hated and, not only that, was extremely sensitive to. Similarly, she didn't like to see anyone drinking too much.

Last of all, he would have to love her family as much as he loved her. To her, family was central to her life almost as much as her faith in God. Jim felt the same about his own family, and he was amazed to find he hadn't made a similar request of God in his own list. In both cases there was no doubting that this standard had been met.

Meditation on all these things revealed clearly to each of them that they had indeed found the one whom God had intended for them. With that assurance now in place, they could consider the future and make plans. Unfortunately for Jim there was still one area of the past that needed to be dealt with first.

Going to the sexually transmitted diseases clinic for a sexual health check and AIDS test was a glaring reminder of past failures. As a Christian since the age of three, there should have been no need for him to be there, had he stuck to the principles he'd been taught so many times in his youth. But as life progressed, with it came loneliness, and with that came alcohol, and on several occasions with loneliness and alcohol came sex.

Greater still came the obligation to confess his mistakes to Maria. He'd already come clean about all the other major areas in which he'd messed up in the past—drinking, drugs, violence, debt—yet none of it had put her off coming back for more. In this instance, though, it felt a whole lot worse. After marriage his body would belong to her, and the thought that someone else had already had the use of it was eating away at him. Only now did God's logic of abstaining make sense. And boy, did it hurt! Even though he'd already had huge insights into Maria's forgiving nature, it lingered that this might be one step too far and result in it being the shortest engagement in history. Either that or cause a wedge between them that might take a long time to get over.

As it turned out, this was to be the last time he'd ever doubt Maria's forgiveness. While she appreciated his honesty when he told her of all he'd done, she couldn't help feel a little aggrieved that he'd contemplated there being an abiding problem developing as a result. After all, if God had forgiven him, why would she not?

Her response left Jim in no doubt she was committed to him one hundred percent. It also gave her an opportunity to expose other areas in her own life that previously had not been divulged. This exercise in soul-cleansing, while extremely uncomfortable, would form an excellent foundation for their marriage.

Nevertheless, Jim still had another problem with his past. Immigration to the United States had certain sexual health requirements that needed to be met and failure to meet them meant that his application would be denied. Even though he hadn't engaged in any form of sexual activity with anyone in a few years, there still existed the possibility that something might yet be lurking undetected. The day he attended the clinic, he was somewhat nervous, and he prayed throughout.

When the results came back negative a week later he cried while repeating his "Thank You's" to God! He thought about how many opportunities there had been where he could have so easily been infected. There was no question God had been merciful to him in either allowing him to avoid picking up diseases from his past encounters or by healing him from any he had. It had been the first test of his faith in God's plan and an indication that his future with Maria lay in America (and not the UK), and with his help, he'd come through it unscathed. The relief was overwhelming.

Not only that, it was one more thing he could include in his testimony when sharing the details of his and Maria's ongoing story with others. Questions of his sex-life were always popular amongst his work colleagues, so it was with great delight he could now inform them he'd been set free from his.

Revealing his Christianity with confidence was a new experience since he met Maria. In fact, his confidence on the whole was increasing, as was his faith. The only downside was that his prayers were becoming one-dimensional as the focus was nearly always on her and their relationship. It was somewhat fitting that between getting engaged and meeting up again came Thanksgiving, and as Maria celebrated it with her family, Jim observed his version of it on his own with the Lord. Both had a lot to be thankful for, that was for sure!

Eventually the time came for his next trip to San Antonio. As he sat on the plane, he tried to imagine what it would be like when at some point in the future he'd be leaving for good. He pictured the sadness on the faces of his family as they said goodbye, and the strange feeling of making probably his last ever flight as a solo passenger. Then he pictured Maria waiting for him at the other end and the smile on her face as she ran to embrace him, and suddenly everything was well again. There was no uncertainty about it. He knew how much he loved her, and no matter what it took to be with her, it would be worth it.

He got a preview of what it would be like when he landed. Maria had come to pick him up from the airport for the first time, and the smile on her face he previously envisaged was even more beautiful in real life! He ran towards her and took hold of her tightly, almost lifting her off the ground as he spun her around in his arms.

"Good flights?" she asked once all the commotion had died down.

"Aye, champion!" Jim replied. Even if the plane had broken in half on landing, it would have been instantly forgotten the moment he held Maria!

Before going to Steve and Diane's house, where he would be staying, they went for a milkshake at a nearby diner and made preliminary plans for the week ahead. Top of the agenda was to buy Maria's engagement ring. He had looked for one for her in the UK, but in the end decided to wait until she was with him so that he could propose to her properly. Also, there were a lot of friends she still wanted him to meet, and some more alone time would have to be built into the program as well. Soon though, the conversation died down to allow them the opportunity to sit and stare in silence at each other and just enjoy the moment—something that distance had cruelly denied them four weeks ago when they made their decision to be wed. The moment was special, and here in each other's presence, that historic decision was now being vindicated. Love, in all its glory, was alive and well between them!

When they arrived at Steve and Diane's, Diane opened the door, and a loud cheer from within greeted them as they entered. She and Steve had a group of friends over for Bible study that evening who had all been made aware of the engagement and were especially excited for Jim having previously met him before. Now as they met Maria for the first time, it was hugs and congratulations all round, something Jim felt would be a common occurrence over the next eleven days of his stay. Once he finally got some sleep, he felt sure he'd appreciate it more the next time.

He walked Maria back to her car and kissed her on the cheek before she drove off. Then he went back inside where he stayed up chatting with his hosts for as long as he could before finally collapsing into bed.

The following evening Maria had arranged dinner at a restaurant with some close friends of hers, Janice and Rodrigo. Rodrigo first met Maria when they worked together for several years in the same hospital, and both he and Janice had also attended the same church for almost the same amount of time as she had. Now, following a change in career, he was employed in a ministerial capacity at the church and would be able to officiate at the wedding should they agree to it, but the main purpose of the get-together was just so that they could meet Jim.

Janice and Rodrigo had helped Maria through all the ups and downs of her life and knew just about all her friends and family. They were very protective of her, and while they certainly knew her well enough to appreciate she was not one to readily make mistakes, they felt compelled to help her make sure for her own sake. In addition, they also ran classes and offered counseling to both engaged and married couples within the church.

Jim sat nervously answering every question they threw at him about himself and his relationship with her. And there were lots of questions! Having jetlag didn't help matters much either. It wasn't as if he didn't enjoy being in their company—he most certainly did—and by the end of the night, he felt as if his good manners and humor had won them over. But as Rodrigo showed how much better he knew Maria than he did, it made him uncomfortable to realize that despite all the time he'd spent reading her e-mails and talking on the phone, he still didn't know her as well as he would've liked. All those hours of research, and it was as if he'd just failed the entrance exam! He wanted to take hold of her hand at the table to give some sort of indication to Rodrigo and Janice that they were in fact close, but he decided it wouldn't be a good idea!

Getting to know Maria is what these trips to San Antonio are all about! he told himself. Maybe it was just the lack of alone time they'd had together that was starting to bother him, or maybe it was another attempt by the voices of doom in his head to question their relationship. Whatever it was he was determined to get as much time in with her as he could this time round.

The subsequent evening was a bit more relaxing. The time spent with Rodrigo and Janice had given him "good practice," as he called it, for when it came to meeting other people who might pose similar questions, so when he got the chance to meet more of Maria's friends he was better prepared. Now he was at a gathering in which her closest friends, David and Angeline, were ceremoniously switching on their Christmas tree lights. It was a happy occasion filled with over-the-top fun, food, and camaraderie, but it was also a chance to show off Maria's dazzling new engagement ring that they'd bought earlier that day.

Jim spent the evening again answering question after question about himself, about how he first decided to come to San Antonio, and about his relationship with Maria. Significantly, he was at last able to spend more time with John. He was able to further establish with John his character, to set out his plans for the future, and allow John to confirm that his favorable first impression of him was indeed correct. But no matter who Jim spoke to, it was all too apparent just how much she was loved and cherished by all who knew her.

They spent a lot of the evening apart. Even though the theme of the get-together was Christmas, it felt more like a party that had been thrown in their honor. As guests took turns at getting to know Jim, Maria found herself the center of attention away from him. She tried to make frequent checks on him to make sure he was all right but each time found him deep in conversation with someone else. His outgoing nature and willingness to mingle was winning over all who were there, and for that she felt so proud of him; and watching her surrounded by so many genuine supporters made him all the more pleased she was his. David and Angeline's opinion was the one that counted most to her, and when she received a glowing endorsement of Jim from them, her happiness was complete.

On the way home, she received a call from her sister Carmen letting her know that their brother Mannie was in town and at their home with his wife Georgia. Mannie and Georgia lived one hundred miles away and weren't around much, so this was a rare opportunity for them to meet Jim. Despite his exhaustion, he agreed to the invitation to go over and so extend his time with Maria. The order of the evening was to be beer and boxing, and even though the beer was not an option, he enjoyed watching the fight, especially since it distracted everyone's attention enough to limit their questioning of him. This slightly displeased Maria, but to Jim it was a good thing, a nice break from having to use his brain too much more! It was after midnight when they finally parted for the night, but it was another successful introduction to someone important and certainly worth the effort as far as they both were concerned.

The late night, followed by an early start in the morning for the church service, took its toll on their energy levels the next day. A week later was to be the church's annual Christmas musical for which rehearsals had been going on weekly since October, but with only a week to go, they were now scheduled for four of the next five weeknights. In anticipation of her involvement in it all, as well as having to work, Maria suggested that they spend the evening apart, in favor of taking the opportunity to get to sleep early. Jim reluctantly agreed and went bowling with Steve instead. Sitting at home, however, she couldn't get him out of her mind so she sent him a text, saying, "How's it going? Are you averaging 250–275? Call me later, if u want…Love you! Me."

"Later" turned out to be 10:45 p.m. Two hours after that, the conversation ended. The regret of the decision to spend one of the precious nights available apart from each other was very much evident, especially when six out of the next seven would be spent at church rehearsing and performing the musical.

Thankfully for Jim, he got a break when the next day he was offered the chance to help out at the musical rehearsals. His responsibility was to position the props on stage in between numbers and to assist in their creation in some cases. On arriving at rehearsal on the first night, he got the chance to meet up with so many more of Maria's choir colleagues and, having previously seen them on TV, it was difficult not to appear star-struck. The church was internationally renowned due to the worldwide broadcasting of its services, so to see them up close and to play a part in something they were staging was like landing a dream job to him. The best part, however, would always be getting to see Maria sing. Even though they didn't get to spend much time together, it was still better than the no time they'd spent on Sunday evening.

Most of the next few days were taken up going with Steve to buy props for the show, but both he and Jim still managed to fit in a round of golf on one of the days and make a surprise visit to Maria with some flowers on another. Maria's days unfortunately were taken up by work. All but one of the evenings were spent at church in rehearsals. On the night off, which was granted to allow the performers a break from it all, it was a chance for Jim and Maria to go on another date.

Maria stopped by to pick up Jim, and they drove downtown to see the fantastic Christmas lights that illuminated San Antonio's city center. For all their splendor, the opportunity to be with each other was more significant, and as they walked along the sides of the river, he turned to her and asked, "Do you mind if I hold your hand?"

"Sure," she replied.

She was just the right height, and her arm was just the right length! It wasn't something he'd included on his list of attributes for his future wife to possess, but he was glad God was one step ahead of him in this respect. Technically, it was the first piece of intimate contact he'd had with her since they'd hugged that night in October, barring a few single parting kisses in the few evenings before, *and it sure felt good!* Now they felt like a couple.

Time constraints meant that the evening had to be cut short. They made their way back to the car and on getting in, paused for reflection on the wonderful time they'd just had. Then, as Maria was about to start the engine, Jim looked at her and said, "I'm sorry, there's something I've been wanting to do all night."

His heart pounding and his body trembling, Jim leaned over and kissed Maria. After their first kiss was over, Maria initiated their second kiss.

They were both speechless. They sat staring out at the parking lot for what seemed like a long time before Jim urged her, "We'd better go."

"I think so," she replied, finally finding some words.

Driving home, there was much silence with a few muffled attempts by both of them at breaking it. In the end it was better to steer the subject away from what had just taken place in the parking lot onto other things.

"So, I'll see you tomorrow night then?" Jim asked.

"Yeah, I guess."

"Cool!"

"Hey, those lights were nice downtown, eh?" Maria asked, taking her turn to say something just for the sake of it.

"Oh, aye, champion!" Jim answered, followed by yet another period in which nothing was spoken. So it continued until they reached Steve and Diane's house.

"See ye tomorrow, then," Jim said smiling.

He kissed Maria then exited the car.

He entered the house and was greeted by Steve who was grinning. "Did y'all swap slobbers then?" he inquired, playfully scrutinizing Jim's face for lipstick marks!

"Naw man!" Jim replied, trying not to blush in the midst of his lie. To a degree, he also felt relieved that Steve's joke masked a kind of indication that it would've been all right by him if he had!

He waited until everyone else went to bed before he made his now-customary call to Maria that night. The good news was that she had managed to obtain the next day off work and would be able to spend another day with him. The call still lasted over an hour—they had lots to talk about!

In the morning, a tired-looking but excitable Maria came to pick him up. Like Jim, she'd spent a great deal of time lying awake replaying their special moment in her head before finally falling asleep in the early hours. Now, just a short while later, she was with him again, thrilled at having just about the whole day to spend with him and full of intrigue at how this one was going to pan out.

First she took him to introduce him to her daughter Jacqueline at a diner close to her house. Jacqueline's husband, Vincent, accompanied her along with their two year-old son, Bobby. Jacqueline had previously exchanged e-mails with Jim following his engagement to her mom, welcoming him into the family and talking to him about all things Scottish, so to Jim, actually meeting her was already somewhat easy.

The breakfast was a success, and everyone got along well. Jim was now acquainted with all members of Maria's immediate family, with the exception of Jacqueline's other two young children. Things were indeed progressing quickly, but with the limited time in each other's company it seemed to be the only way. And with that time being so enjoyable to both of them, it didn't seem to matter.

After breakfast, Maria decided to take him to the church's country retreat in the Texas hills where it all began for her earlier that same year. Although it was winter, it was still a warm and sunny day that made even the bare landscape more beautiful than it already was, and Jim was only too pleased to accompany her.

Upon arrival they checked with the manager of the property that it was okay to continue, and he confirmed that it was. They left the car at the entrance and, hand in hand, walked slowly through the surroundings. There were no urges to do anything else except enjoy each other's company and breathe in the clean country air as they surveyed the magnificence of God's creation. Feeling closer to His presence, they sat down on a rock by the lake and prayed that He would bless their relationship.

Afterwards they drove a few miles down the road to where there was a picnic bench beside a river. Maria proposed an exercise in which they wrote down some situations or emotions that might crop up in the upcoming months, then find a Bible verse to cover it. The idea was that they would then exchange cards and have something to look at in the other person's handwriting to encourage them through such an event should it ever arise. Moreover, it was the chance to study the Bible together, which she'd longed to do since hearing him share so much of it in the e-mails he sent her. Jim was only too happy to oblige, and it not only proved to be worthwhile from a spiritual point of view, but it also helped them in discussing the future of their relationship.

At the end of the assignment, Maria produced her diary for the upcoming year to see if they could come up with a date for their wedding. They both knew that delaying their marriage beyond the end of another year was not what they wanted, nor did they believe that they needed more time to be sure of their commitment to each other, so it seemed like the right thing to do under the circumstances. After all, God had ordained it, so why wait too long?

October seemed to be the perfect month. Their wedding could coincide with the church festival that Jim's family so desperately wanted to attend again. The problem lay in that it hadn't yet been confirmed on which weekend in October the annual festival was going to be held, nor were they assured of the church being available on the date of their choosing. Furthermore, they were not one hundred percent certain of the immigration filing requirements. They would have to take a leap of faith.

They prayed before they selected the date, and they prayed again afterward. Informed guesses and reasonable estimates as well as their trust in God for it to come to pass led them to choose as the day of the wedding: October seventeenth.

Now it was on! They were able to go back to their friends and begin spreading the word. Even though it was not yet confirmed, their heartfelt belief that God had led them to that date was enough for them to speak out in faith that it would take place as predicted.

The weekend passed, and the church musical was a success. Jim made sure his props were correctly placed, careful not to be distracted by how gorgeous Maria looked in the choir behind him in her red blouse and sparkling necklace he'd bought her for the occasion. Maria sang her heart out like never before, buoyed by the joyous emotions bubbling away inside her. Their story was spreading among the church staff and choir, initiated primarily by people wanting to know whom the Scottish guy was who was helping out. And Jim was already starting to feel at home.

"Home" was a big issue for him. During his childhood he'd moved house with his family seven times and, since leaving his parents, another ten times. It wasn't that he had itchy feet, it was just the way things worked out. The continuous upheaval not only became boring, but it also became depressing. His biggest desire was to find a place in which to settle down, a place he could feel safe and accepted by the people around him, a place to finally call "home." Now here in San Antonio for the sixth time, and being with someone as wonderful as Maria, it was starting to feel like he'd at last found that idyllic place he so desperately craved. "Please, Lord, let it be so!" he prayed.

On Monday, the day before he was due to leave for the UK, Maria picked up Jim and took him to her house. The day off work had been booked in advance, and the plan was either to watch a movie or just sit and relax and enjoy each other's company, which they were able to do for a little while. Unfortunately there was the matter of the immigration paperwork to attend to.

Jim was a paperwork guru! His father had taught him when he was younger how to carefully and accurately address all that was being asked for before proceeding, and his previous employment working in an office had helped consolidate what his father had taught. The responsibility for most of the forms lay with Maria, and he wanted to be with her to pass on his expertise as she filled them out. Leaving it until the last day of his stay, however, was not the best way to spend their final few moments together.

The forms took just over three hours to fill out, but the experience was not all bad. Just being able to sit so close to each other at the same table was not a common occurrence. In the middle of it all were pauses for more kisses and a chance for Jim to sample some of Maria's cooking for the first time.

Once they'd finished, they sat staring in silence for a while at the completed documents as the magnitude of the situation began to sink in. They not only had a wedding to plan, they also had to build into it immigration procedures and red-tape, all of which would require large amounts of time and money. Research had indicated the whole immigration process could take around nine months, so it was imperative it was completed within that time in order for Jim to move to America with plenty of time to spare before the wedding (which was ten months away). There could be no hold-ups, no requests for further information, no bureaucratic ineptness. It *had* to go smoothly! And so they prayed, "Dear Lord, maker of heaven and earth, we come before You offering our utmost praise that You have brought us this far and that You are at the head of our relationship. We ask that You oversee our immigration process from the safe delivery of these forms to letting our case be dealt with in a prompt manner and by someone who is highly capable at their job. We ask that our case will be looked upon favorably and that all the information we have supplied will be sufficient for it to be passed on to its next stage without further requests for information or clarification. And that all this will take place within the parameters of time that will enable us to be married on October seventeenth, the date we believe You have given us for our marriage to take place. Your Word says there is nothing too hard for You! We therefore hold tight to Your promise and look forward to seeing Your hand at work in our situation. With thanks, in Jesus's name, amen."

At the end of it all, Jim described to Maria his longing for a place that he could call home and how, with her in his life, he felt he was getting closer to it. He played her a song from his mp3 player in which the lyrics described the singers' joy at finding their true love and the way it made them feel like they were now at the home they so desperately wanted to belong to. As the song played, Maria gazed lovingly in his direction. Her smile was broad, and her eyes were wide. Jim caught sight of her out of the corner of his eye but pretended he hadn't noticed as he rambled on over the top of the music for a while longer. When it finished, he asked, "What do you think?"

"I think I love you," she replied.

The look on her face was mesmerizing, and Jim struggled for a coherent response. "Uhh, wanna see my tattoos?" was the only thing he could come up with trying to divert his attention away from the physical attraction he was now experiencing.

He and Maria both realized that being Christians did not exempt them from wanting to extend their activities beyond kissing. Fortunately they had the presence of mind to recognize the existence of the sexual tension within the room and turn away from it.

"We'd better get going now I suppose," Jim said.

"I suppose!" Maria replied.

They picked up Isaac from school and then headed back to Jim's where they said goodbye. They spent the rest of the day apart; Maria stayed at home with Isaac while he did his homework, and Jim went with Steve and Diane to look at neighborhoods in which the Christmas decorations and lights were so prominently and magnificently displayed. He felt guilty at having abandoned them most of the week and had promised he'd spend his last night in San Antonio there with them, but while he was with them in body, his mind was somewhere else with Maria.

The next day Maria came to the airport to see him off, wearing the Scotland soccer shirt that he'd bought her for Christmas with her name printed on the back. She gave him a card, and she made him wait until she was gone before opening it. Then, before the plane was due to board, she kissed him goodbye and waited until he was out of sight before allowing herself to cry. Saying goodbye as friends was difficult enough. Now it was excruciating.

Jim managed to hold himself together until he opened her card. In it she wrote in the center, "You are …" Surrounding those words, she had scribbled all the different ways she could think of to describe what he meant to her, and on reading it he found it hard to compose himself. Later she sent him a text, which read, "You are so special to me, my love! We can do this. Be strong. My heart belongs to you now and always will."

Trying to hold back his tears, he reflected on all they had achieved in the past eleven days and held fast to the notion that one day he'd never again have to go through the painful experience of having to say goodbye.

His thoughts turned to God, and he thanked Him for all that had happened then reaffirmed his trust in Him that everything would work out.

And then, in his final farewell before boarding his plane to London (and as the onboard music system fittingly played a song called "Miss You Like Crazy"), he replied, "Goodbye my precious, beautiful, wonderful, adorable, awesome, treasured blessing! You are loved more than you'll ever know!"

Chapter Twelve

After declaring his love for Maria, Jim always made sure he had another trip arranged ahead of time. That way, as his next visit to San Antonio approached, he had another one to look forward to. Knowing when he'd be coming back again also softened the blow at having to leave.

His next trip was booked for February, just over two months away. Ten weeks between visits didn't seem that long on paper, but with Christmas, New Years, their joint birthday, and Valentine's Day sandwiched in between, it would no doubt seem longer.

He wondered how the next trip could ever top the last one. He'd gotten to see more of the *real* Maria—the relaxed and fun Maria—and in her first e-mail to him after he left, she asked if he was happy with what he saw. "Are you sure you're okay with my goofiness?" she asked. He wasn't just okay with it, he *loved* it—although he tried to think of the instances she meant in which her behavior could have been construed as goofy and couldn't count that many. The good thing was that his next visit would last nineteen days, so he'd get plenty more opportunities to look out for it! *Man, it's gonna be a long wait!* he thought.

While Jim whined about being in the freezing cold UK again, Maria was still living off the euphoria of his visit and her gratitude to God. In another message to him she wrote,

> Praise GOD! It makes me want to serve Him and love Him so much more! If only everyone could feel what we are feeling, what a happy place this would be. Again, it's the best thing this side of Heaven!!!

Her Christmas spirit was also rejuvenated. The next day she and Isaac set about decorating the house, inside and out, with decorations and lights. She spent hours choosing gifts and cards for everyone she knew, undeterred and unaffected by the long lines and discourtesy of others at the stores. She bought Christmas music to listen to, and her joy was made complete when a friend sent her a card addressed to Maria, Jim, and Isaac.

She watched with excitement the envelope containing the paperwork for the immigration authorities disappear behind the post office counter, knowing the whole process was now officially underway. She considered what might happen if it were to be dealt with in less than nine months. *Would we be able to get married sooner?* she wondered.

She bought two books on marriage and planning a wedding. She called to book the church for October seventeenth and was told that the date was provisionally available. She also set up pre-marital counseling classes for her and Jim to attend next time he was in town. Dreams of her wedding day filled her head both day and night, and she took great delight in sharing them with her equally-as-excited fiancé.

All in all, she was just happy, and nothing could change that! Even though Jim wasn't there with her, the simple fact that he was in her life would still make it the best Christmas ever!

Underneath the misery of being back home, Jim pretty much felt the same. Any time he felt his mood drop, he retrieved the card Maria had given him at the airport and pored over the loving sentiments contained in it, the aroma of the perfume she'd sprayed on it filling his Shoebox apartment each time. He also had more snapshots now in which he could study her face and reminisce on the wonderful moments surrounding when they were taken.

The thing that amazed him most was that he'd found someone who loved him as much as he loved her. Each time he showered Maria with love and affection, she'd return in kind with some equally adoring words of her own. It was becoming almost like a competition to see who could love the other the most!

Similarly his love for God was now at the highest level it had ever been. He'd watched in the past as Maria demonstrated her love for him through her earnest worship and now found himself imitating her in his own. On Christmas morning he attended church with his family and praised God with everything he had. And as he watched the children show off their presents to the congregation, his only regret was that he couldn't show off the precious gift that God had given him in her.

After church came Christmas dinner, and after dinner came his phone call to Maria. Two hours later he rejoined his family for what would be their last Christmas together for a few years, on account of his impending move to America, before retiring to his room to send her an e-mail. No matter how much had been covered on the phone, there was always more they could discuss in writing!

Maria's time with her family was consequently delayed by two hours. She had dinner with most of her family at Dan and Carmen's house then spent the evening with Jacqueline, Vincent, and their three children.

"So will you be moving to Scotland, Grandma?" asked Belle, her five year-old granddaughter, with panic in her voice.

"No, he's gonna move over here," Maria reassured her.

"What will we call him?" asked Alvin, aged six, the oldest of the three.

"I don't know, I haven't thought about it," Maria replied.

"So if you're Grandma…and he's going to be married to you," said Belle, "then that makes him Grampa! I'm gonna call him Grampa Jim!"

"Me too!" said little Bobby.

And so Jim became a grandfather! He always knew he'd inherit that role, but it wasn't until Maria told him of her conversation with the children that the reality of it sunk in. He couldn't wait to meet Alvin and Belle, and the idea of being their grampa actually appealed to him. In a silly attempt to get used to it, he gave his colleagues at work permission to call him Grampa Jim, but few took him up on the offer.

It was something else to reflect upon as the year drew to a close. He'd started it off single, lonely, and for the most part, unhappy; now he was finishing it engaged to be married, about to become a stepfather and grandfather, and set to move to America.

He pondered a request of God he'd made near the beginning of the year that he would be free from his airline industry job by Christmas; now he was glad that God had refused his request since he'd need all the money it would provide him for his emigration and wedding.

And he told Darius that it was the first time in his life that he didn't want a year to end—it had been that good! The amazing thing was the upcoming one would no doubt be even better!

At midnight on New Year's Eve, he called Maria to wish her a Happy New Year. He was partying, alcohol-free, at a local bar near his house along with his family, but the cost of calling from his cell phone didn't matter as the sound of her voice was all that mattered.

No amount of alcohol in the past ever made him as happy as he was now! He called her again at 6:00 a.m. to coincide with the start of the US New Year, and once again the sound of her voice was able to override the downside of this time having to get up early after the late night. *Even if it was only her voicemail he reached, it was still good!*

Maria spent the last few hours of the year visiting a friend in hospital before going to the special late-night service at church. At the hospital she shared the story of how she and Jim had met and how just five months later they were engaged to be married. Her friend and his wife shared how they too had fallen in love based on a mutual desire to worship God and were engaged after just two months of dating. They warned her against being defensive and worrying about what other people thought, reminding her that since God had put her and Jim together, then everything was going to work out fine. They also questioned the possibility of the wedding taking place sooner than October. "If only we could!" Maria sighed, pointing to the immigration obligations that first had to be settled.

Two days later she received a letter from the IA (immigration authorities) responding to their petition for Jim's visa. It stated their case number and basic information about how the case would be dealt with. It also gave instructions on how to find out the expected length of time it would take to be processed based on the volume of other petitions.

She e-mailed the details to Jim who couldn't wait to get on the website, hoping maybe for some welcome news. To his horror, the new guidelines stated that the initial petition would be reviewed within eight months. Assuming that there were no further questions or information required, it would then be sent to another location in the US for "additional processing" before subsequently being passed on to the American Embassy in London.

Once it reached London, there would be more documentation and forms for Jim to submit; and upon receipt of these, the expected time before hearing anything else was stated at three to six months. It could then take a further month or two before a medical and an interview were granted and the visa ultimately issued.

In other words, the whole process could take anywhere up to sixteen months. They now only had nine and a half.

Before Christmas, Maria had proposed that in the new year, they ought to adopt the biblical principles of fasting into their schedule as a means of giving their prayers an extra boost. In practice, fasting was a new concept to Jim, but he'd always been aware of how great men of the Bible, including Jesus, had applied it. He was in favor of Maria's idea and was willing to go along with it, but now, faced with such a desperate problem, he was *more* than willing—they both were!

Despite it all, Jim remained confident that God had absolutely decreed that their wedding should take place on October seventeenth. They received word from Rodrigo that the church's annual festival that year would take place on the weekend commencing October 23 and that their wedding plans could now be confirmed.

Maria's suggestion concerning fasting was that they undertake it the first week of every month, starting in January. A host of excuses, mainly from Jim, meant it would not start until midway through the second week!

Before an alternative solution was found, Maria took their situation to Heinrich, one of the elders in the church, for prayer. After she explained it all to him, Heinrich said he felt a peace and a genuineness about the situation, and he believed that God would indeed cause all things to work out for good because of their faith. When he finished praying, he advised her that they should fast one day per week until the wedding. She hadn't told him of their existing intention to fast, nor of their struggle to begin it, so once again God had intervened on their behalf, this time through Heinrich.

She added up the number of days in which they'd be fasting, and it came to forty days. When she told Jim, he erupted with glee; not only was forty days a significant total within biblical parameters, but also he recalled a forty-day Bible study-plan he'd read the previous year and how he'd received a major answer to prayer at the very end of it. While there was no fasting involved in that instance, there was no doubt in his mind it was significant.

They decided to follow Heinrich's instructions and proceeded to fast one day each week. In order that they were in harmony with each other, they devised a list of things they would adhere to when making their prayers known to God. It read as follows:

> To keep God/Jesus/the Holy Spirit the focus of our lives, hearts, love, attention, worship for the rest of our lives.
>
> For continued prosperity in health, wealth, and spiritually in both our families.
>
> For direction, favor, and supernatural anointing with regards to planning the wedding from the receipt and prompt processing of the visas, to the details of the invitations, the ceremony, the reception, and our wedding night.
>
> To allow God to use us for His glory!
>
> Most importantly, *to trust God* in all areas of our lives, to let God be our God and not limit Him to what we are able to imagine.

Armed with such seemingly strong indications that their wedding would go ahead as planned on October 17 as well as a potent means of ensuring they would come to pass through God's intervention and reward of their devotion, they viewed the year ahead with confidence and that there was nothing to be worried about.

Maria set about planning her year ahead and the dates she would need to take off work. One of the things she'd previously discussed with Jim was the possibility of her coming to visit him in the UK. Even though the wedding was probably going to cost a lot, Jim felt there would be much overall benefit to be had if she had an insight into his culture and background before they were married. Plus it would be a much-needed break from work and other things, which she probably would otherwise not have taken. As such, she penciled in a week in July and began looking at airfares.

The first item on the calendar was their birthday on January seventh. Unfortunately she couldn't allow herself the day off work for it, and neither could Jim. Being born on the same day, albeit ten years apart, was not something they ever read too much into, but it was always going to be special. As with so many events throughout the year they were unable to spend together, visions of how extra-special it would be the next time round were enough to keep them going. In his absence Jim surprised her by e-mail with a collage of photographs showing himself as a child until the present day. It didn't compensate for having the real thing with her, but it was a wonderful substitute.

Next on the agenda for Jim was an extended stay in Germany with work. Usually the short-haul nature of his airline's business meant he'd always end up back at home, but on rare occasions there were trips away. He took with him the card Maria had given him at the airport and photographs to show her off to his colleagues. Every day at work, he would be quizzed time and again about his relationship with Maria, and time and again he would gush with excitement about it. He was so happy and didn't mind sharing it, and neither did his colleagues it seemed.

Not only was he excited, but his family was, too. Joining him in the faith that all would go ahead as planned, they began checking their passports and booking their flights to San Antonio for October. Ruth searched for places she could send them on their honeymoon as her gift for their wedding, and both she and Jim began planning an itinerary of things to do with Maria for her pending visit.

Meanwhile Maria was experiencing mixed emotions about the wedding itself. On one hand was the thrill of planning it, and on the other was the realization she'd have to do most of it herself. With Jim abroad and only in town for short periods, they'd also need to apportion that brief time together between doing what they liked and doing what was important. For now, though, it complicated matters having to choose things like the reception venue, the invitations, the décor, and so forth without him present.

Choosing her dress, however, *was* one thing she could do on her own and one that brought her much satisfaction. She reflected on a recurrent dream she used to have before she met Jim in which she was dancing for joy in front of the Lord wearing a white dress. Her dream was now coming true right before her eyes, and it was hard not to cry as she tried them on.

Good news for Jim was that his driving license was reinstated, and he was able to move out of The Shoebox and back in with his mother and sister. It would give him his first opportunity to rid his possessions of those he'd be unable to take with him to America, and he was ruthless in carrying it out. Nonetheless, it was still difficult saying goodbye to items he'd hung on to for years for no other reason than sentimental value, and he knew he'd have to do it again before he left for good. It brought with it an awareness that his possessions would soon not be the only things he'd need to say goodbye to.

At his new accommodation, Ruth allowed him the use of her car as much as possible and gave him rides to work whenever she needed it for herself. She also refused to charge him rent and allowed him the use of her landline to make free phone calls to Maria. As a result he was able to save money and book another two-week trip to San Antonio for the end of April.

Being back with his mother and sister, Jim began to feel like he'd been indirectly sited into a place of preparation. Dealing with correspondence and carrying out the heavy work around the house on Ruth's behalf and building snowmen and dancing and playing around with Stacey was like being the head of a household that had previously struggled without one for some time. In amongst it all, he couldn't help but think that God was readying him for times to come; from living on his own to being a part of a family again was an adjustment he'd later have to make when he got married. Watching his mother perform household chores gave him insights as to what it was like to live under the same roof as a woman, and making allowances for Stacey's youth-like tendencies would be good practice for becoming a stepfather to a teenager. Despite the frequent strain of it all, having his mother and sister to help him through the lonely moments was an invaluable benefit.

In addition, the move seemed to bring with it an acceleration of time, and it wasn't long before he was on his way back to Texas. Every last space in his suitcase was crammed with the first of little things he planned to leave over there in anticipation of his future move, and the journey over was crammed with thoughts of his wedding. With less than eight months to go, this would be his first involvement in its planning, and, unlike most men he'd heard of, *he couldn't wait*!

Chapter Thirteen

Making the events of the ten weeks between visits more complicated was the whole gamut of emotions that accompanied them. Reflections on things past, present, and future intermingled with the desperation of being so far apart, and the strength of the red tape obstructing their union. Life was certainly not dull.

Top of it all was the new-found excitement of the physical side to things they'd uncovered since their first meaningful kiss. Maria was still overwhelmed at the timing of it.

The physical aspect of any relationship was what had been keeping her back from committing herself to anyone in the years leading up to now. Fear of the actions of the other party, fear of the unknown, fear of herself. She'd already dismissed a relationship with Jim before she met him the first time; her decision was not based solely on the long-distance element, but rather her lack of desire to be involved with someone again on all levels. Having a male companion and a father-figure for Isaac would be nice, but that was about it.

When Jim came along, she was astounded that his main reason for wanting to meet her was the way she worshipped God. The more she spoke with him by e-mail and telephone, the more his character seemed to back up his motive. His knowledge of the Bible, the sincerity in his own worship, the way he respected her on their first date, and the way he exacted nothing more than a hug so long after he first professed his love for her were all contributing factors to the way in which her love for him grew.

Jim backed up her faith in him on more than one occasion stating that the thing he wanted from her more than anything else was that she simply allow him to love her. "Let me love you," he pleaded, desperate that the unique brand of love he'd wasted on so many in the past would not be rejected again by her. His was a love from the heart and not of the eyes.

Now the fact that their first kiss came *after they were engaged* was just staggering. There could be little doubt their love affair was built on anything other than respect and a mutual belief in God. In one e-mail, she wrote,

> My love, I am so blessed to have you in my life! The things you endured, the promises you hung on to, the waiting and the listening to the prompting of the Holy Spirit, and your obedience through it all are all awesome signs of a leader, one whom I am willing to love and support and follow!

And now, after creating such a strong spiritual and emotional foundation, came the revelation that a physical bond existed between them. The news was, of course, much welcomed, but it also opened the door to feelings previously subdued and topics never before discussed. It would be difficult not to build upon their kiss in future moments together, but after much deliberation on the subject, citing personal experience and biblical teaching as reference, they determined resolutely that it would not be extended beyond kissing until their wedding night.

Discussing the physical side to their marriage led them to consider other aspects of being married, which they hadn't dwelt upon or even encountered before. In the past they'd never argued on anything, much less fought, so the issue of conflict was brought up. With both having such easy-going personalities, it was hard to imagine there ever being a problem in that area, and even though it was tricky to talk about, to know in advance how the other would respond in such a situation threw up some welcome information.

Similarly, on the issue of finances, there seemed to be little cause for alarm at things never before revealed. Both were in agreement on the importance of tithing their income to the church, and the amount of charitable donations they regularly made failed to take the other by surprise.

Most other emotions made their appearances naturally as the weeks passed by. Besides the happiness of being so much in love, the most prominent one was still the dejection at being separated by five thousand miles of ocean and the inability to comfort the other in person when times were tough. Maria had several such instances, especially with work, which was causing her to work long days, sometimes in excess of twelve hours. She looked forward to speaking with Jim on the days he was able to phone her just so she could vent her dissatisfaction on someone else. While he was happy to be that outlet for her, it only added to his irritation at not being physically present to hold her in her times of need.

Jim was taking it upon himself to worry about the immigration side of things. In spite of the various confirmations there were along the way, he still chose to take his eyes off God, surrounding himself with the bigger picture and ignoring His role in it all. Each time there was movement in the IA's processing timelines, it was either very little, or it had changed for the worse. As time marched on, the outlook became increasingly bleak, and he became increasingly despondent. Until one day, concerning the situation, he was sure he heard God say, "I want you to praise and worship Me right now and hereafter like you would at the moment when you find out you've got your visa. In other words, picture yourself with the visa in your hand right now. Imagine how elated and ecstatic you're gonna be and how you're gonna thank Me over and over and over—that's how I want you to praise Me between now and then: with everything you have!"

He remembered back to that first morning when Maria first told him she loved him, how he was crying with joy, how immovable his smile was, and how he spent days just thanking Him continuously.

God went on to say, "*That's* how I want you to worship Me on a daily basis!"

Perhaps it was just his imagination, or perhaps it was something he'd heard on Christian television that he'd somehow paraphrased in his mind. Jim chose to believe it had been God speaking to him. To him, whatever it was, he decided to act upon it because it certainly *sounded* like it was something God would say and was in line with biblical teaching he'd previously received. It was enough to turn his fears into cheeriness again—for a while at least.

Those fears were soon replaced by other things such as fear of not being able to find work and fear of being a lousy role model to Isaac. Maria soothed and reassured him as best she could that no matter how things turned out, her confidence in him would always remain, but to Jim they remained problem areas that were hard to let go. Equally, when she confessed to feeling overly-guilty for removing him from his beloved family, it was difficult to otherwise convince her that their future together was now more important.

Added to fear came frustration—frustration whenever anyone would ask questions they didn't know the answers to, the most common one being, "What happens if the paperwork isn't processed in time?" Other questions along the lines of "Are you still getting married?" and "Is the wedding still on?" although good-natured or intended in playful jest, were becoming more and more grating. Jim always tried his best to respond cheerfully and assuredly, but so often the questions would linger in his mind, causing more inner debate. Maria was better at dismissing them after she'd given her answer, but it was hard not to feel betrayed when the meal-ticket issue eventually reared its ugly head from some who'd initially given their support. The concepts of pre-nuptial contracts and divorce were even put to her. God's response of, "Do you think I can't handle all this as well?" was comforting but again soon forgotten as the overwhelming hurt began to eat away inside.

Jim's continued reliance on nicotine gum was made all the harder to give up. Additional factors such as the long, cold winter, the delays and cancellations on all his flights caused by the snow, and the forced sale of his pet snake, which he loved and he'd had for five years, only added to the dilemma of being unable to be with Maria, who in herself was becoming increasingly burdened with the stress her workload was contributing to her existing woes. At one point Jim even researched the possibility of visiting her just for two days, such was the desperation of wanting to be together (in the end, cost and common sense overruled it). And once again Maria was reminded by someone at church of the teaching that "before great victory comes great turmoil"—more welcome encouragement, which unwittingly would soon be cast aside.

Amid all the gloom and despair, however, were some happy events. Maria attended a dance recital, evoking memories of her white-dress dream, as well as other special events being held at the church over the festive period and beyond. Jim kept alive his dreams of one day attending the church with her on a regular basis by watching her sing on the DVDs that Steve had given him and through the weekly services, which were broadcast on the Internet. The subject of marriage was being given more attention as well, not just at church but on Christian television programs all over, or maybe it just seemed that way to them, but it certainly felt like a timely endorsement from God of their plans to be married.

The e-mails continued to flow, and the telephone calls could now also be more frequent as a result of Jim's move to his mother's. The more they spoke, the more comfortable with each other they became. Cards were received at Christmas, their birthday, and

Valentines Day, for which they compiled long lists of all the individual things they loved about each other.

The biggest highlight in it all was when Maria booked tickets for her and Isaac to visit the UK in the summer. To her came the excitement of going overseas for the very first time, and to Jim and his family, it brought with it the excitement of planning her vacation to make sure she'd have the best time imaginable.

The price of the tickets was much more than they'd expected, but when Maria assured Jim it was insignificant next to the chance to see him again, he almost cried. It wasn't because it was the trip of a lifetime, it wasn't because she longed to see the UK and all it had to offer, it wasn't even because it was a much-needed break. It was because she wanted to be with him! Not that he needed it, but it was yet more confirmation of the love she had for him, and for that he just couldn't contain his emotion.

Aside from the cost, the tickets also had to be booked in faith that her work would allow her that particular week off work. Policy stated that vacation time could only be requested less than three months in advance but at the risk of an increase in price, she was forced to book early.

Ultimately, despite all the emotions their time apart was bringing, it would have to be faith that came out on top. It would have to be the one ingredient to override all other emotions if they were going to succeed in their plans to be married on October seventeenth and the one thing that ought to be permanently on their lips as they spoke out their intention for them to succeed. At times it was hard to come by, but there was no denying its need in order for them to prevail. Faith in God, faith in his Word, and faith in his miracle-working power.

Faith!

Chapter Fourteen

Before Maria's UK trip came the first of two more Texas visits for Jim.

"Hey, bro, welcome home!" Steve exclaimed when Jim walked through the door. "Has it really been three months?"

"Two and a half!" Jim corrected him, with a smile.

"We missed ya," said Diane. "But then we miss you when you're here, too!" she said, hinting at the amount of time he spent with Maria on each of his stays at their house.

It was true: the more times he came over, the more time he was spending alone with her and less with them. It hadn't escaped his notice either, and he did feel guilty about it, but both Steve and Diane were not ones to underestimate the importance of their short time together, especially now with so much planning to be done.

Nevertheless, he still tried to balance his time between the golf course and the bowling alley with Steve, his times around the dinner table and the TV with Diane, and all the other times with Maria. No matter how hard he tried, though, Maria always ended up getting the greater share!

"What's y'all's plans for this time round?" Diane asked, looking at Maria who was also there, and hoping that Jim hadn't taken offense at her previous remark.

"Well, we gotta do some more stuff for the wedding. We're gonna go fishing, not this weekend but next, gonna spend some time with the grandkids hopefully–" Maria said.

"Oh, and we've got *pre-marriage classes* to attend!" Jim added. It did sound as if he were being facetious, but in reality he was looking forward to it. His mind had told him he already knew all there was to know about Maria, but just to see if he'd missed something was an exciting prospect!

"Well, hopefully y'all will have a night spare so's y'all can come round for dinner?" Diane asked optimistically.

"Sure, that'd be nice," answered Maria. She, too, was starting to feel guilty and at that point made a mental note to somehow offer them something that might make up for all the outrageous kindness they'd shown her and Jim. Both of them had tried to do it in the past, but modesty and humility on the part of Steve and Diane would not have them allow it. This time she was determined to get them something they would accept.

"Aye, champion!" said Jim. Diane loved to cook, and he loved to eat, so it would always be a no-lose situation as far as he was concerned!

Maria left him to his hosts and drove home. After she got home, the night ended with the obligatory lengthy phone call between her and Jim before tiredness eventually overtook excitement and sleep became necessary. They had nineteen days in which to enjoy each other's company—the longest they'd ever had—and it felt like all the time in the world.

They would soon find out, however, it wasn't all the time in the world. The days and weekends of the duration of Jim's stay elapsed quickly, and soon he was on his way back to the UK again. Back to the tail-end of the cold British winter and the start of the next six weeks apart, back to more of the same mixed emotions, and back to the need for even greater faith as the wedding date inched closer with no further word from the authorities.

In between was the "best visit ever!" as Jim put it. Every time seemed to be better than the last, but then the love they shared was becoming stronger each time, and it possibly just gave that impression.

In actual fact he spent most of his days hanging around waiting for Maria to finish work. Some days he had a longer wait than others as she involuntarily demonstrated how the overwhelming demands of her work were taking a toll on her personal life. The issue of always finishing beyond her regulation time became a thorny one for Jim who felt she was being abused by her employer and almost became a cause for their first fight. Fortunately it was able to be put on ice until it arose during the pre-marital classes they attended whereupon Rodrigo could act as mediator.

The classes covered various subjects and were a mandatory pre-requisite to being married at the church. They provided an excellent means to ensure both parties were ready for the commitment ahead, and neither Jim nor Maria were fazed at having to take them. With so much emphasis placed on the importance of communication, it felt easy to open up to one another; after all, communication was all they had to bridge the distance in the long periods spent apart. Indeed, as they made their way through everything the course had to offer, they found little they hadn't already discussed in their many hours of e-mailing and phone calling.

On the topic of work, however, Jim continued to struggle. Aside from his issue with Maria over her working too much, it highlighted the fact that his skills were not readily suited for easily finding employment in the US. His first career, which had ended ten years previously, was as a tax consultant, and not only was his knowledge now considered obsolete, the tax laws in the UK were somewhat different than in the US. After he left the tax industry, he became manager of licensed premises, and his various employments over a period of five years had seen him managing bars, restaurants, and even a hotel. They also contributed greatly to much of his troubles with alcohol, and he now no longer wanted to be around it. Finally he had become a flight attendant, but residency restrictions upon his eventual emigration to the US, for various reasons, would not allow him to continue in that career. Even so, the idea of working away from Maria for any length of time during their marriage was not something he ever wanted to happen again. Going back to school to study for a new career was not an option since neither he nor Maria could afford the tuition fees nor the means to survive on only one income while he obtained his degree. He would therefore have to find work in a new career, starting from scratch, and hope that within a short period of time it would be able to adequately finance their distant plans to have a baby. In other words, it would require faith!

"More faith!" said Jim, already struggling to find enough for their current situation.

The subject of sex, once married, also threw up its share of struggles. Both Jim and Maria found it difficult to discuss without conjuring up images in their minds of what it eventually would be like. Since their kiss in December, the physical aspect of their relationship had made its way to the forefront of many a conversation, but with their vow to remain faithful to biblical teaching in direct opposition to it, it was certainly bringing about its fair share of difficulties, both in the classroom and beyond. In some ways it would have been better had the physical connection not been established in the first place, choosing instead to trust God that He'd already included it as part of their overall relationship package, but now that it had, it was difficult to let go. Happily, there was no suggestion of it being an issue *after* they were married, but in the meantime, it would have to be simply put on hold, just like so many of their other plans, until the future.

"More waiting!" said Jim.

As much as the classes were for their benefit, they also gave Rodrigo the chance to not only find out more about the stranger his close friend was marrying but also to ascertain the extent of their love for each other. He knew Maria too well to know that she would not be willing to take on such an enormous risk on someone were she not completely sure they were for real, but his mind was put firmly to ease when he observed them in an exercise in communication.

The object of the exercise was to establish how relaxed the two were in each other's close proximity. Each had to take it in turns and talk for three minutes about their plans for their future life together, and neither they nor the listener were allowed to look anywhere except into their lover's eyes. Repeated glances elsewhere would be an indication of discomfort.

As Maria started, Jim found it difficult to look anywhere *but* into her eyes! Her soft American accent was enough in itself to keep his attention, but the love her eyes revealed as she spoke was mesmerizing. *And that beautiful smile!* he thought to himself. As far as he was concerned, he could do this for an hour!

Likewise, when Jim began speaking, Maria gazed at him transfixed. His accent was also endearing to her but insignificant next to his blue eyes, which captivated her. Even though neither of them were aware of what the other was saying, the chance to sit and stare at their future spouse made it their favorite part of the whole course. Rodrigo too was impressed at their evident affection.

As the classes drew to a close, Rodrigo prayed a prayer of blessing over them and expressed his utmost belief in their future success as a married couple. He arranged for a certificate to be made up and for their October seventeenth-booking to be changed from "provisional" to "confirmed."

"We're gonna get married!" said Jim with authority as they walked from Rodrigo's office for the last time.

"We sure are!" said Maria.

They turned to look at each other and with overwhelming joy, laughed loudly as they came together in a long embrace.

It was one more thing they could tick off their mental list of things to do ahead of their wedding. Jim would later compile such a list, but for now everything was being stored amid the innumerable thoughts wildly circulating in both their brains.

One other such thing on the list was to decide on the music for the reception. Maria had heard through a friend at church of a fantastic band who regularly played at a restaurant in town, so it seemed like a good idea to go and check them out. She came to pick up Jim and took him back to her house where he waited while she got changed. Ricardo was in town that weekend, too, and keen to accompany them, along with her sister Carmen.

When Maria reappeared from the bedroom, Jim was awestruck! She had on a black dress that reached her knees, and her long hair was straightened the full length of her back. She wore an enchanting fragrance, and her make-up was immaculate. He'd never seen her looking so beautiful in all their time together, and to be out in public where everyone could see him with her was going to make it the best night ever!

"You look…gorgeous!" he said.

"Thanks," she replied, and smiled.

"Now you look…perfect!" he continued, referring to her smile.

Moving towards her, he placed his hands on her shoulders and placed a small kiss on her lips. She smiled all the more as he withdrew. She felt like a princess, and to Jim she not only looked like one, but he was also going to make sure she was treated like one too.

Arriving at the restaurant with his aunt, Ricardo was also suitably impressed at the transformation in his mother's appearance.

"Wow Mom, you look great!" he said emphatically as they headed across the parking lot.

Inside they were fortunate to be seated relatively quickly in spite of large crowds who had gathered at the restaurant. After ordering, Maria and Carmen made a trip to the restroom together, and Jim was left with Ricardo at the table.

"So, just wanted to ask you," Jim began, "how do you feel about me and your ma getting married?"

"She seems happy enough, that's all that matters," Ricardo replied.

"No, but are *you* okay about it?"

"I guess. It's a bit too early for me to say. I hardly know you. You seem cool enough though."

Ricardo was never one to give much away. As a highly educated and intellectual young man in his early twenties, he had a lot to be admired from an academic standpoint, but to Jim, his personality had yet to be firmly established. It was as if his brain were contemplating another matter at the same time as he was talking, and it always left Jim curious to find out what it was.

"I'd like it if you could accept me. In fact, I was gonna ask your permission to marry her before I did so, but the moment just kinda happened quickly, and I didn't get the chance. I had your e-mail address from a while back, so I was gonna use that," Jim went on. "So, sorry about that! But how you feel is still important to me."

"Just don't hurt her!" Ricardo warned him. There was nothing hidden behind *that* statement!

"No! Don't worry mate!" Jim anxiously countered, almost like a child in front of an angry parent. "That's the *last* thing I'd *ever* do! I promise you that with all my heart! Honest!"

"That's cool."

And with that they went back to listening to the band who had just begun playing. Ricardo's face went back to its usual composed state, and Jim breathed a sigh of relief that at least his response wasn't an outright rebuke.

When Maria and Carmen returned, the impression at the table was that there had been silence since the moment they left.

"You boys okay?" Maria asked them both.

"Sure," said Ricardo, as if nothing had happened.

"Aye," said Jim, still trying to regain his composure.

After they'd finished eating, Carmen turned to Jim and asked, "Aren't you going to ask your bride-to-be for a dance?"

"Oh, I'm not much of a dancer," he responded, ashamedly. Noticing a trace of disappointment on Maria's face, though, he quickly tried to rectify the situation, "I guess I could give it a try, mind you!"

Turning to Ricardo he asked, "Do you mind if I dance with your ma?" It wasn't the same as asking his permission for her hand in marriage, but it made him feel like he'd gone a little way to making up for it.

"Sure, on y'all go."

He elegantly took Maria's hand and led her onto the dance floor just as the band began playing a slow song. Not sure of where to put his hands, she helped him out by establishing her own stance first. With one hand on his shoulder and the other around his back, she moved in close until her hair pressed lightly onto his cheek. He took in a deep breath, savoring her sweet aroma as he did so, and let his feet begin moving.

It was true he wasn't the best dancer in the world, and she had to correct his rhythm more than once. But as he began to relax, his nerves were soon replaced by pride—pride from being seen with the most beautiful woman in the room—and love.

Back in the UK, Jim reflected on the time he'd spent in San Antonio. It had felt more like an expedition than a vacation in so much as he'd spent more of it scoping out the geography and studying the culture than simply appreciating it like the tourist he used to be. The city had lost its newness, and for the first time, he hadn't bothered with visiting its attractions and hotspots.

He'd been introduced to so many faces he'd need to remember for the future instead of previously only having to give a one-time acknowledgement. He'd finally met his two other future step-grandchildren and spent more time with the rest of the immediate family. Together with Maria, he'd gone fishing with Isaac and his friend Matthew and had gotten some more photographs as well as some fantastic memories. Neither would he be able to forget their times spent at the movies, in restaurants, at church, in class, with Steve and Diane, and with his old friend Kevin and his wife, Sandra, with whom he'd managed to hook up again.

And his familiarity with Maria had increased to the point that they could concern themselves with doing essential things rather than fun things. In effect, instead of it being the leisure destination it was to him in the past, San Antonio was now beginning to ever so slightly feel like home.

Maria, too, was enjoying the reminders of his trip. Her friends were constantly asking after him and expressing their commiseration that he'd had to leave. More began to offer their services towards helping with the wedding in whatever way they could, and it was now gradually taking shape. Prayers were regularly being offered concerning their immigration difficulties.

A photograph of her and Jim now sat proudly on her desk at work. She carried a poem he'd written specially for her in one of the times they were not together. And her Scottish teddy bear—a gift he'd brought with him at Christmas—he'd sprayed with cologne, the scent of which greeted her each time she lay down.

Over the next few weeks, there was more to feel good about. Maria became a grandmother for the fourth time as Jacqueline gave birth to a baby girl, naming her Heather (which Jim liked because of its Celtic overtones). He was also encouraged when, in another phone call to Jacqueline, he got to speak with five year-old Belle whose parting words to him were, "I love you Grampa Jim!"

That felt good! he said to himself.

Maria was buoyant when Ricardo decided he wanted to come with her and Isaac on their trip to the UK. She was further uplifted when the time off work was granted by her employer. "Yet more confirmation of God's blessings on us!" she told Jim.

Another great moment for her came when she finally decided upon her wedding dress and purchased it. She had discussed it with Jim beforehand and found out his ideas of how he thought she might look; now she believed she'd found the perfect dress to suit both his and her tastes.

Jim's dependence on nicotine was slowly waning, helped along by their weekly fasting in which he chose to forego his gum in place of time spent in prayer.

His guest list of friends and family from the UK who wanted to attend the wedding had increased to sixteen people, and all had booked their flights. It deeply moved him to know that there were sixteen people who were willing to go to all that expense and give up their time just to see him get married. It also brought about panic in Diane when he teasingly asked if they could all stay at her house.

Steve felt deeply privileged when Jim called and asked if he'd be a groomsman at their wedding. To Jim it hardly seemed enough, but since Darius already had the best man position, it was the highest honor left he could offer Steve.

Stacey was ecstatic when she was confirmed bridesmaid and advised she would be escorted down the aisle by Steve. She had developed a deep affection for him since meeting him the previous year, and this news was almost as good as the wedding itself to her.

Ruth was overjoyed when Maria asked if she could call her "Mom" and just as happy when she sought her opinion more in matters concerning the wedding. When Maria e-mailed her pictures of her wedding dress, her levels of excitement were off the scale! Both she and Jim picked out a list of possible hymns they felt appropriate to be sung at the ceremony, and she also booked a honeymoon for them in California for the day after the wedding.

For Jim and Maria, life would have been bliss were it not for the fact that they were so far apart from each other. It became especially hard when Maria's friend, whom she'd visited at New Year's, passed away, and once again Jim could not be by her side as she struggled to come to terms with her grief.

Issues within each of their employments were also bringing their own strife, and the problems at Maria's work began affecting her health to the extent that she was ready to quit. Jim did his best to encourage her, but with family issues and a wedding to take care of causing more stress, she was eventually forced to turn to medication to ease it.

For Jim it was a return to the skies the day after his return from Texas, and even his first day back was beset with problems. A fault in the airplane had caused it to be grounded until a new one became available, and a three-hour delay ensued. When it eventually did take off, they ran out of food, and the passengers ran out of patience, choosing to voice their complaints in his direction. A couple of weeks later, on another trip to Germany, he decided to hospitalize one of his crew members after she violently hit her head and required emergency first aid, which he and a colleague had to administer. In a separate incident, he shut a door on the fingers of another colleague, bruising them severely. And then came the ultimate insult when a letter was received from a passenger threatening legal action against the company for a misunderstanding over an incident dating back six months in which he was the one at fault in her eyes. Two meetings later with the company's attorneys showed she had a flimsy case, but to Jim it was the ultimate insult in his ever-increasing dislike of his job.

Even so, the problems were this time outweighed by their love for each other, which was still escalating daily. In an exchange of e-mails, Maria described more of how exactly her love had developed for Jim at the beginning of their relationship and did her best to explain those periods in which her hesitancy in fully opening up to him had been apparent. She expressed her amazement at how, even at such an early period, he was able to pick up on the way she was feeling and how he was even better at it now.

She loved that about him—there was nothing she could hide from him. Such was his love for her that it could discern when she wasn't being truthful to her feelings, and she promised she'd do better at disclosing them in the future.

Being the object of so much adoration and love of the sort he continually poured out on her was just something she'd have to get used to. She'd experienced it in the past but never to this extent. Nor did she find it easy to accept based on her own perception of herself, which was radically different from Jim's. As far as he was concerned, she was the most wonderful and most beautiful woman on the planet, and his love for her had become unconditional. And in his most powerful e-mail of all to her he wrote,

> Maria,
>
> I have seen unconditional love in action, close-up, twice in my life. The first was the love my Granda' had for my Gran (my other Gran—not Granny, whom you met). For all she was a lovely, lovely, born-again Christian lady, she treated him like something you'd step on in a cow pasture. Yet he continued to serve and adore her right up to the day she died (around twenty-five years ago). He hardly ever retaliated nor left her,

even though he had strong Biblical grounds for doing so. And even after she died, his house was like a shrine to her: her pictures were everywhere, and he kept everything she ever wrote.

The second was the love my mother had for my father. Again, she had strong Biblical grounds for walking out and never going back. But to watch her at my father's bedside in the last days brought more tears to my eyes than watching my father himself. She visited him every day in hospital, read the Bible to him every day, prayed with him and over him, and nursed him better than any professional ever did.

Both those unconditional loves finally died two years ago, and I thought I'd never see it in action ever again. That is, until I met you.

I made it my goal, and my promise to God, that if He ever blessed me with a wife so special that I would love her with a love so strong it would make both those loves I mentioned above seem pale in comparison. I also knew that it would take someone so unbelievably special to be the recipient of it to the point that I was starting to do just that: disbelieve. Disbelieve that someone that special actually existed. I thought they all died off in the fifties with the films that so fantastically portrayed them. Yet still I clung on to the small shred of hope that there was one, just one maybe, left in the world and that I would find her...

... and I did. Praise God, she does exist! She's you!

Maria, my love for you is unconditional. You have to know that. And I've been waiting so long for the opportunity to tell you it, too.

If (God forbid) you ever become terminally ill, or lose all your limbs, or suffer burns to your whole body...or even something as simple as just becoming old...know that I will love you no matter what. And I will never leave you.

> Want to know why I love you in that way? It's because you're you. You're my special blessing, my gift from God, my beautiful princess…you're mine. You're everything to me. You've brought the romantic music back into my life, and put the word "love" back into my vocabulary. I will love you with an unconditional love that cannot be matched this side of Heaven; not in a movie, nor in anyone else's relationship. I say all this, knowing in full confidence that I have the love to back it up, by simply saying these two words to you: I promise!

When he'd finished writing, he heard God whisper in his ear, "I love you more than that!"

He began to weep uncontrollably. He was reminded of a verse in the Bible that says "he who has been forgiven much, loves much" and recalled his past in which he'd done the most despicable things yet still God had forgiven him them all (Luke 7:47, paraphrased). He now loved God more than ever before in his life, and here it was being reflected in his love for Maria, as proved by this verse. It was a small insight into how much God loved him unconditionally.

With Easter—his favorite time of year—having just passed and still fresh in his thoughts, he reflected on the cross of Jesus and His unconditional love for mankind and applied it to himself. It brought to mind a chemically-dependent friend of his who too had been saved from an early death through his new-found faith in Jesus Christ and who often could be seen crying in church, just like he did, as he remembered all he'd been through. To Jim, the only form of worship worthy enough of his gratitude was through tears, and as he thought of Jesus, and then of Maria, his tears were flowing freely. Then when he finally composed himself he finished off his message:

> I guess I'll never understand why He loves me like He does—His love is WAY too big to understand, and He wouldn't be God if it was able to be understood. But there's still one other thing I guess I'll never understand either: why you love me the way you do, too. I could go back and read every e-mail you've

sent me, and ever will for that matter, and I'd still never know the answer to that. But then likewise, if I could understand it, then you would no longer be that what you are to me every day, and that is simply this: Special!

Chapter Fifteen

With five months to go until the wedding, Jim made what he considered to be his last visit to Texas. Still clinging to faith and God's promises that everything would work out fine, he reckoned the next time he would be coming over would be for good.

His visit was just as eventful as all the others in the past had been and unfortunately passed by seemingly as quick. He and Maria did as much as they could together concerning the preparations for the wedding; they were even able to find time to have professional photographs taken, and on his last night they were pleased to finally entertain Steve and Diane at an up-market steakhouse.

Upon his initial arrival into San Antonio, Maria took him to his usual place of stay at Steve and Diane's house, stopping off first at a nearby restaurant for a quick bite to eat. There Jim produced a present he'd brought for her and had wrapped specially in romantic paper: a book. Thinking it was another Christian book he'd possibly recommended her in the past—and one she'd struggle to find time to read—she tried her best to look excited as she peeled off the sticky tape. Nothing could have prepared her for what she uncovered though.

Jim had taken all the e-mails they'd sent each other from the very first one up until just before they'd gotten engaged and had them made into a hardback book. It had a photograph of them together on the front and another on the back, some narrative he'd composed imaginatively describing its contents on the rear cover, and a dedication page inside, which read, "To Maria, with all my love, to remember forever how God brought us together and how our relationship began…"

Struggling to contain her emotions, she hugged him for over a minute. When she eventually let go, she wiped her eyes and struggled to force words past her enormous smile. "I take it you like it then?" he asked.

She kept the book close to her, even after Jim returned to the UK, and news of it spread among her friends. When John heard of it, he asked if he could borrow it to show at his upcoming meeting of Bible study group leaders, so impressed was he at the depth of love Jim held for her to go to such lengths to show it. She allowed him to take it, under oath that its contents remain confidential and would not be read by neither him nor anyone else. He agreed, and soon news of her relationship was spreading further.

John showed Tim, the choir director, and relayed to him the story of how she and Jim had met and fell in love. Tim showed the rest of the choir at a practice, and a clamor to get a closer look ensued, but John made sure it didn't leave his hands. Some asked if they could buy a copy while others jokingly asked Tim if they could be moved to the front row so they might have a shot at attracting a mate!

In a rare turn of events, Maria was not there that night. The following week, however, she was present and was asked to recount the story in front of the whole choir, which, despite her shyness, she managed to do. Some of those closer to her heckled her, shouting things like, "Tell them the bit where…" and, "What about the bit where he…" while others gasped in amazement, and some shed tears at all the little things that took place along the way in bringing the relationship to where it was now. In all her nervousness at being on display, she remained faithful to stress God's part in it all and His continued involvement to date. Afterwards, Tim and the rest of the choir prayed over her and her situation, making her glad she'd told them despite the discomfort she felt in so doing.

Meanwhile, preparations for the wedding were gathering pace. Jim drafted the invitations. Maria met with the church's wedding coordinator over the order of the ceremony, and she picked out the bridesmaids' outfits and had an initial fitting of her own dress. She finalized reservations at a restaurant for the rehearsal dinner the night before, booked a hotel room for her and Jim for the night itself, and arranged for Mannie to take them to the airport the following morning for their honeymoon, and they both were thrilled when the band to which they'd danced along with in February cancelled their existing plans in order that they might play at their reception. Jim was enjoying every minute of it and tried hard to distance himself from the stress that Maria was undoubtedly feeling, but still he couldn't help wishing he could do more.

Unfortunately he couldn't distance himself from the stress of his immigration. It was approaching six months from the time the original paperwork was submitted, and still they'd heard nothing. The IA's response times for their particular type of visa petition indicated it should have been already dealt with, yet Maria was unable to talk with anyone when she tried to follow up by phone.

Jim remained positive in his answers to the questions others continued to ask, yet the pain was gnawing away at him. When people became persistent in trying to make him see the distinct possibility of his visa not being granted on time, he was eventually forced into making contingency plans.

The plans involved proceeding with the wedding but holding off from signing the official documents that legally bound their union. That way they could consider themselves married in the sight of God and still proceed with their wedding night consummation and honeymoon arrangements. The legal side of things could later be taken care of at another small registry office affair once the visa was ultimately granted.

Both Jim and Maria sought advice from those more knowledgeable concerning the biblical aspect of such dealings, but in the absence of a definitive answer either way, they had to rely on their own convictions that it would be acceptable to God.

Another downside would mean Jim having to leave Maria in the US after the wedding and return to the UK until everything was sorted. Having to leave her those times while she was his fiancée was excruciating enough, but to have to leave her behind as her husband would be intolerable. If it was going to take over a year, as was stated at the outset, there was no telling *how* long he'd have to wait to be permanently with her, and even the thought of it was enough to make him ill.

The plans could work. Even so, it was still grating against his faith and all the declarations he'd made that everything would turn out fine. He also felt as if he were betraying God by disbelieving His Word and all the things He'd already told him concerning the matter. And that *really* hurt!

Maria was choosing not to worry about it. She had convinced herself that God would indeed grant them the miracle they needed so that none of the back-up plans would be required. Her problems lay with those select few who continued to emphasize their prejudice that Jim was a fraud. While their sharing of their beliefs was not all that difficult to ignore, it was impossible not to listen to and only added to her existing feelings of sadness that he couldn't be there to prove them wrong.

In a bid to escape from things, Jim decided upon a few days away and chose to visit Israel. The year before he'd expressed his lifelong desire to visit the Holy Land to an elderly Israeli lady named Crystal whom he met on one of his flights, and she responded by giving him her address, inviting him to visit her anytime. Grateful at her overwhelming kindness and trust in his character, he remained in contact with her by e-mail, and when he wrote asking where best to stay she offered him a room at her house. With Darius being able to get him incredibly low flight prices, the free lodgings, and this being his last opportunity to vacation on his own, he decided he had nothing to lose and took off on vacation.

Jim was a seasoned traveler and had visited many countries in the past, but without doubt, his time in Israel now ranked high at the top of the list! Not only did it have its religious significance in regard to his Christian beliefs, but it was also a country of exceptional beauty. Crystal's energy, despite her age, and her hospitality were other outstanding factors in making his trip so memorable, and the three days he spent with her were nowhere near long enough!

He was able to communicate with Maria using Crystal's computer and pass on his unparalleled excitement in e-mails that seemed to go on forever! He visited Jerusalem, Bethlehem, Nazareth, and the Sea of Galilee, among others, and took notes of his tour guide's comments, which he then extensively relayed to her at night in his messages.

Before his trip he pondered, with a tiny trace of regret, the fact that once he was married, he'd no longer be able to go on any more crazy solo trips abroad. Now the fact that she wasn't there made him realize how much he missed her and how he never wanted to do it again. How he wished she could share in his adventure, and reading about it, she felt the same.

Nevertheless there was still her upcoming visit to look forward to. When he returned home, it was business as usual for Ruth who had been frenetically planning her visit ever since it was first breathed. She'd already had a shower added to the existing bathtub and replaced the floor tiles; now she had her sights firmly set on a party to celebrate their engagement and to welcome Maria and the two boys to the UK.

Stacey was equally as excited at their arrival, even allowing the use of her much-guarded bedroom for Isaac and Ricardo. She had seen her bridesmaid's dress online and couldn't wait to talk to Maria about it. She also filled many photo frames with pictures of her brother and Maria and placed them strategically in his bedroom one day while he was out.

To Jim, their enthusiasm was commendable but exhausting!

The visit gave everyone the perfect opportunity to clear the house of junk and Jim the chance to sell more of his things he wouldn't be taking with him to America. They were given the free use of a stall at the town market and were able to successfully raise money, which they subsequently donated to charity. Sadly for Jim, it was a day spent watching treasured items, on which in some cases he'd previously spent a small fortune, go for pennies in comparison. If nothing else, it taught him a lesson in value.

Maria had one more overnight stay at the church's retreat in the countryside before her UK vacation. It was a chance to get some rest and relaxation ahead of her overseas trip. For sure she wouldn't be getting any while she was there: Jim's pre-planned itinerary of her visit had already guaranteed her none! She wouldn't be getting any after it with the wedding to arrange.

It gave her another opportunity to reflect on how things began. The time when Steve first approached her there with news of the

Scotsman who was "madly in love with her." She remembered the next time, exactly a year ago, and how her friend Julie had persuaded her to accept her feelings for Jim and to be open to what lay in store. Then she recalled the moments spent there with Jim and all the other wonderful things that had taken place since she first met him outside the church—too numerous to count. There was no denying it had been quite a year!

In all the ever-changing times between those periods in which they were together, one thing remained constant: love. The need to spend hours on the telephone and in front of the computer typing e-mails was still just as strong and as fresh as it was when it all started. It never became a chore. And apart from the logistical side of things, the biggest difficulty they faced was finding new ways in which to express their love for one another.

As Jim contemplated for himself the year gone by, he composed an allegory, which he sent to Maria, offering his view on things past, present, and future. It was a powerful piece of prose, inspired by God, and summed up their whole relationship. It was the only way he could think to add to all the other I love you's and expressions through contact and gifts they shared. It became his anniversary present to her...

Once Upon A Time...

> ... there was a young man who learned to appreciate art at an early age. He loved to look at paintings, and as he grew older, he began to invest in them, all the while being on the lookout for what he regarded as the perfect painting.
>
> His search took him far and wide, but after a while, he soon began to discover that his quest was not going to be as easy as what he thought it would be when he first started out. Sometimes he would invest in paintings only to find that after closer inspections they were flawed. Other times he would view paintings on show but found he did not have enough

money to buy them. And then there were times where he would view, or even invest, in such paintings but later find out they belonged to someone else, which often brought him much trouble.

After a while he became very despondent and substituted his love for art for cheap wine and liquor. Sure, he still liked to look at paintings, but his own appearance was repulsive to sellers, and he found himself only able to afford the cheapest sketches from the dirtiest outlets. He soon gave up on his dream and spent many years in illness and misery.

Years later, however, he began to have various encounters with the king's servants in the land. They offered him care and medicine to help him overcome his problems and even persuaded him to consider resuming his quest. And sure enough, once he became well enough, he set off again with a renewed sense of optimism and faith.

After a while he received an invitation to a feast at one of the king's houses in an overseas land. While he was there admiring his surroundings, he noticed a painting of extreme beauty. He hadn't gone specifically to look at the paintings, yet this particular one stood out among the rest, and he could not take his eyes off of it.

The man, to his astonishment, was permitted to meet with the king, and in one of his conversations with him, he asked him if he would consider selling him this beautiful work of art. The king, however, was aware of the man's previous illnesses and refused to part with it for fear that he would not treat his painting with the care and respect that it quite obviously deserved.

Undeterred by the king's reluctance to relinquish his prized artwork, the man returned two more times over the next nine months to the king's house in the far-off land. Each time, he met with the king and presented himself free from his illnesses, which caused the king to have a change of heart. The king arranged for the man to have a private viewing with four of his subjects, and the man was overwhelmed to discover that, even up close, the painting appeared flawless. He later returned with one of his own friends to show him this glorious sight, and his friend agreed that it was indeed a thing of great wonder. His friend persuaded him that he should make the king an offer, and after a little while longer, the king accepted.

The man was so overjoyed he returned to his family, crying and announcing to the whole world that he had found his perfect painting that he'd spent his whole life looking for! His family and friends shared in his happiness, and some even agreed to help him out with the cost. He took photographs of his painting and decorated his house with them, and he would always carry one around with him everywhere he went in order that he could show others. The man even spent many nights making calls to the king, thanking him over and over for his agreement to sell but more importantly for his trust in him to look after it.

However, strict export regulations in force meant that the man would be unable to bring his new possession back to his house in the land in which he lived. He would have to move to the far-off land in order to be united with his painting and move in to the building in which it was kept. He decided that having spent his whole life searching for his treasure that it was a sacrifice he was willing to make.

And so he began to sell all of his possessions, and, one-by-one, he said goodbye to all his friends and then finally his family. The king had authorized his immigration to the far-off land, and soon after his arrival he was given the title deeds to his painting in a public ceremony before many invited guests, including the king himself. At the unveiling of the painting itself at the ceremony, the man discovered that it was even more glorious than he'd ever remembered or imagined! As he took the painting home that night—still amazed by how one painting could contain so much splendor—he gazed at it with proud satisfaction and uttered the words he'd been longing to say all his life: "My masterpiece!"

As the years went by the man never stopped loving his painting. In fact, he became more and more attached to it every day and continued to send thanks to the king at every opportunity he had. He treated it with the utmost care and respect he had promised the king—all the attention it truly merited—and he never ceased to show it off to all he knew whenever he could. And yet he never lost sight of the trials and troubles he had to endure before he was finally permitted to be at-one with his painting.

As the man reached the end of his days, he pondered one more time on the joy and pleasure his one painting had brought him throughout his whole life. He smiled as he reflected on how he never saw the need to buy another painting after he'd found his treasure. He never became tired of it, and every day he noticed some other outstanding feature of it that to his delight he'd never discovered before.

Then one day the king came to the man's house and invited him to come and live in the palace and to bring his painting too. This the man was only too happy to accept, and he took hold of his masterpiece...and followed the king to his new home.

Chapter Sixteen

"Welcome to the UK!" Jim exclaimed, as first Isaac and Ricardo walked through the arrivals door, followed by Maria. "These are for you!" he joked, handing the bouquet of flowers he'd bought for her to Isaac. He hugged all three individually, saving the biggest one for last for Maria before showing them all to his car.

"Good flights?" he asked. "Any problems?"

"No, your directions were perfect to the letter," Maria replied with a smile, referring to the four pages of step-by-step instructions he had e-mailed her the night before.

The thrill of being overseas for the first time was overshadowed, in the case of the two boys, by the overnight flight and lack of sleep, and it wasn't long before they dozed off in the back seat. For Maria, the whole experience was just *too* exciting and enough to keep her wide awake as they drove back to the house. She was enthralled by the various shades of green of the English countryside and the height of the trees along the roadside. As such, Jim decided to take them home via a different route—through winding country roads and small villages—and although it made their already-long journey even longer, Maria loved every second of it.

The town where he lived was surrounded by countryside and made a good impression on his guests when they went exploring it later in the afternoon. Beforehand though, came the reunion with Ruth and Stacey, who were somewhat excited at their arrival.

"*Maria*!" screamed Stacey as she came charging out to meet them at the car.

"Let her breathe!" said Ruth as she followed behind her, referring to the tight grip she had around Maria's neck.

"That's okay," Maria said when she eventually let go.

"How *are* you? Was your journey okay? Did you sleep? Was Jim's driving okay?" Ruth asked, not pausing for much breath herself. "And this must be Ricardo? Hey! Welcome! And Isaac—*so* good to see you again! You all—sorry, I should say, 'Y'all'—must be so tired! Come in! Welcome!"

"Just how I remember her—always happy, always moving!" Maria said to Jim as they brought up the rear of the line back into the house.

"This is Ailsa, and this is Angus," Ruth went on, presenting them all to two of her friends who'd come down specially from Scotland to attend the party she was throwing for them the following evening. "*Auntie* Ailsa!" said Ailsa, laughing, correcting Ruth's introduction. She wasn't really an aunt, but with her motherly nature and the fact that she'd known Jim since he was born, she liked to assume the title.

"And you remember Samantha, yeah?"

Thankfully, that was to be all the greetings for now. There would be many more over the course of the weekend to look forward to, but in Ruth's opinion they were still being broken in gently beginning with only five.

Following their venture into town, they returned to the house, and Isaac and Ricardo caught up on some sleep. Maria was determined not to allow her first experience of jetlag get the better of her and stayed up talking as more people came to the house to meet her. First there was Jennifer, another friend of Ruth's from Scotland whom she'd picked up from the train station while they were in town; then came Martin and Granny; then Uncle Fred and Aunt Rose, Granny's brother and sister-in-law; and finally two more of Ruth's English friends, Howie and Joan.

At night they all went for a meal at Jim's favorite Indian restaurant before Maria's exhaustion began to show, and she was finally allowed to go home to sleep. Before retiring, she and Jim took advantage of their small escape from the crowd to gaze into each other's eyes again and remind themselves of what they'd been missing. The new surroundings to her became irrelevant again; as long as she was with him, she was happy. And right then she was very, *very* happy!

The next morning Darius arrived early with his friend Boaby whom he'd brought with him from the north of England. Ruth laid on a full English breakfast for all her guests, and Jim set about polishing off those items from the plates of the Americans that they didn't find too appealing!

After breakfast he took Maria and the two boys on a train trip to another city in an attempt to escape the ever-increasing crowds of people converging at the house. He showed them buildings of grand architecture and beautiful parks in which trees of great size were in abundance. They were even fortunate enough to observe a cricket match taking place in the afternoon, although the general consensus was that it was not the most exhilarating of sports.

Returning home, they found more people to be introduced to. The party Ruth had organized did not start until evening, so she had arranged a pre-party gathering of those who had traveled a great distance and those whom she wanted to become better acquainted with her future family before they would later have to circulate among so many more. She expected around one hundred people to attend the party itself and wanted to make sure no one was disappointed. Unfortunately the pre-party lasted too long, and the only ones disappointed were those left waiting at the main event for their arrival, including those who'd volunteered their services to perform some of Jim and Maria's favorite songs who'd been singing since the time they were supposed to get there.

Nonetheless, the party was a huge success. Almost as many as were invited turned up, making it a healthy crowd that Maria, Isaac, and Ricardo spent the first hour individually meeting. There was more food to enjoy, a live band playing for a while, and a DJ playing tunes to finish off the night. In between, Stacey entertained everyone by singing an Elvis Presley song on stage into the microphone. Ruth even arranged a segment in which a friend of hers taught line-dancing, Texas-style, to those who were brave enough to give it a try.

The date also happened to be July Fourth, so the family's friends and church had helped decorate the hall in as much American memorabilia and artwork as they could find or create. Most guests turned up wearing the colors of the American flag or cowboy attire; some even went as far as dressing up as Hollywood stars and action heroes. Ruth did her best to look like a 1920s showgirl while Granny surprised everyone by turning up dressed as Granny Clampett from the TV show *The Beverley Hillbillies*. Jim wore a shirt Steve had given him that was completely made up of stars and stripes, while Maria wore a t-shirt in the style of the Scottish flag. The irony was appreciated by all who were there.

The occasion was marked by a friend from church who perfectly sang the *Star Spangled Banner* while Jim and Maria, together with Ricardo and Isaac and Ruth, stood on stage listening proudly by. Ruth then gave some thanks to those who'd helped put together such a special evening before passing the microphone to Jim. Addressing the assembly, he said, "I'd like to add some thanks of my own. To all those Ma mentioned who helped put together such a momentous occasion—on behalf of Maria and I—the biggest thank-you imaginable!

"I'd like to thank all of you for coming. Some have traveled a great distance and at great expense just to be here tonight to mark our engagement, and that is just overwhelming to us both. But not just to them, to all of you. We'll never forget you. Our only regret is that you all can't be there in Texas in October to see us get married, even though you are all officially invited! If you think I'm happy now, just wait til October!

"I'd like to thank my Ma for her part in tonight's proceedings. All the stress and hard work she endured in inviting you all here and the lengths she went to ensure it was as much fun as possible. So thanks, Ma; I love you!

"I'd also like to thank Ricardo and Isaac, here, for welcoming me so much in to their family and for coming over here to visit and for meeting so many people in the one evening! Thanks guys, I love you both, too.

"But finally, I'd like to thank my beautiful, beautiful fiancée. For all the things you've come through and sacrificed just to be with me, for all the risks you took and continue to take concerning my immigration to America, and for agreeing to be my wife, making me the happiest and most blessed guy on earth. You know, I once heard your pastor describe his wife, saying, 'All the rubies in the world could not afford to buy the dust from her feet!' Well, now I know what that means because I feel exactly the same way about you. I love you, Maria, I love you so much! My biggest thanks for tonight is to you—simply for being *you.*"

As the band subsequently played, the pair warmed up for their wedding by dancing a slow dance to Jim's favorite song, "What a

Wonderful World." The world was indeed altogether wonderful—he had his prized possession back in his arms again, and he was letting the whole world know just how much he loved her.

Maria too felt special—Jim's speech echoed in her mind, and the feel of his face pressed gently against hers left her feeling like the most cherished woman in the world. As she looked around and saw how much he was liked by others, she felt sure she was going to cry. She didn't want to let go of him; not now, not ever.

As the night drew to a close, they both reflected on how good it had felt being the center of attention and on the receiving end of such warmth and affection from all who were in attendance.

"It feels like we've just got married!" Jim said to his church pastor and good friend, Gordon, at the end of the celebration.

"Yeah, just remember you're not though until October!" he told Jim with a wry smile.

At church the following morning, the warm welcome for Maria and her family continued. Their presence was announced from the platform, and the flags of the world that regularly adorned the inside of the church—representing the respective nations from whom its listed members originated—for one day only were now joined by ones from Scotland and America.

Following church, Jim's whole family went to lunch with Maria and the two boys, together with all those who'd come down from Scotland. Afterwards they had an invite to meet up with Pastor Gordon and his wife, Suzie, at their house, but with the sun shining and a little time to spare ahead of it, Jim drove Maria to a local park where they sat beneath a tall tree and watched the squirrels.

"So, are you enjoying yourself so far?" he asked.

"Oh yeah!" she replied.

"Goes by quick, doesn't it?" Jim went on.

"What does?"

"The vacation I mean. Here we are on day three already; only four more full days to go."

"Try not to think about it, I'm not!"

"I'm trying not to. It's not easy when you're having such a good time, though. I never thought I'd enjoy being in England so much! Just goes to show wherever you are, I'm happy!"

"You're not suggesting we stay here instead, are you?" Maria tested him, knowing full well what his answer would be. The idea of her moving to England had already been discussed and dismissed out of hand, but his reaction made her laugh every time it was put to him again.

"No chance!" he said.

"What about Scotland then?" she asked him further, referring to their impending trip up north planned for the next day. "What happens if we like it there?"

"Just…No!"

"You're so funny!" she said, laughing.

"And you're so adorable!" he said forgivingly and placed a kiss on her lips. There wouldn't be many opportunities for him to do that over the course of her stay, not with so many other people wanting to be a part of their every move. Having such a unique story that so many people were interested in gave them an almost celebrity-like feeling and made it difficult to find time to themselves.

They left the park and headed to the home of Gordon and Suzie. Gordon and Jim had become close since the death of Jim's father two years prior. Before becoming a minister, he had been a highly successful professional soccer player, which meant he and Jim had another common interest besides their love for the Lord. He had even played in San Antonio during his time in the American Soccer League towards the end of his career over twenty years ago. In a previous conversation, Jim asked if he'd mind filling his father's role whenever he needed someone to call upon, and he felt honored to assume the responsibility. He was his pastor, his father-figure, and most importantly to him, his friend.

Jim and Gordon regularly met for coffee, so he had already heard lots about Maria and how special she was to him. Aside from that, Suzie and Ruth were good friends as well, so there was already a close bond between the two families. It meant that Jim was not at all apprehensive at being interviewed by his church leader. But, even if the close relationship did not exist, he still would not have worried since his confidence in Maria as a person was so great.

Despite Jim's assurances, Maria was slightly nervous at meeting such an important figure in his life. To her it was her turn to meet the parents, even though she'd already met them briefly at the party the night before.

As both Gordon and Suzie welcomed them into their home with warm embraces, it wasn't long before she began to relax. Gordon spent much time with Maria, comparing the San Antonio he remembered with what it was currently like. He and Suzie had already decided they would be in Texas for the wedding, so they spent much time discussing the itinerary, where they would be staying, travel arrangements, and so forth.

"And how's the immigration stuff coming along?" Suzie asked.

"It's not!" Jim replied with a strained look on his face.

"What happens if it doesn't come through in time?" she asked. Jim had already discussed his enforced contingency plans with Gordon one afternoon over coffee, but he went through it all again with Suzie.

"Whatever happens, there'll still be a wedding in October," he said.

"It *will* come through in time, though," Maria added with gentle confidence. "God will make sure of it!"

"Amen!" both Gordon and Suzie said at the same time. A person of faith was someone they'd always hoped Jim would end up with, having seen him so often with the wrong ones in the past. Now their joy in his choice of mate was made complete by her statement.

They prayed over them and waved them goodbye. "See y'all in October!" they called after them through the open window as the car left their house.

"They are just so wonderful!" Maria said to Jim.

"Aye, the best!" Jim replied, as a touch of sadness overcame him at the thought of leaving yet more people behind who meant so much to him.

On the way back to the house, Jim decided to take Maria to a pub right in the heart of the countryside. They ordered a soda and sat outside, surveying the green landscape, the horses in the fields, and the rabbits hopping around just a few feet away. It was such a romantic setting and with the rest of the pub's clientele choosing to remain inside, they took advantage of it by holding hands and reminiscing over all that had happened in bringing them to where they were now.

"I love you," Jim whispered.

"I love you, too," Maria responded.

The next three days they spent touring Scotland with Isaac and Ricardo. They set off early on the Monday and headed for Glasgow, where Jim grew up and went to school. Arriving at lunchtime they deposited their luggage at the guesthouse where they'd be staying and went out sightseeing.

He had predicted that it would be raining when they got there—it rained *a lot* in Glasgow—and when they got there, it didn't disappoint! The views of the city from its highpoint were hampered by the dark, grey clouds that hung low over the tops of the buildings and the rain that was blinding their vision. As such, the sights they set out to see were somewhat restricted.

Fortunately for them it cleared up by evening, giving Jim the chance to take them for a drive up the steep hillsides that faced the town where he grew up. There were green pastures, streams and waterfalls, tall trees, and amazing views. Jim's stories of his youth and his knowledge of the area only succeeded in causing Maria to feel all the more closer to him.

"If you think that's nice, just wait til tomorrow!" he said, hinting at the even greater beauty the further north of Scotland had to offer and which they'd be seeing the next day.

He wasn't exaggerating, either. The next day took them deeper into the heart of Scotland, where the hills became mountains and the streams became lochs and the scenery was simply breathtaking! A quick stop for some tourist shopping by Loch Lomond was followed by a longer stop amid the huge mountains of Glencoe.

Ricardo and Isaac took off up the side of a mountain with Maria and Jim in pursuit. It wasn't long, however, before their youthful edge saw them disappear from view as Jim's fear of heights kicked in at around two hundred feet, forcing him and Maria to retreat back down to the bottom. They sat down on a mound of grass, still a good distance from the car park where a solitary bagpiper was demonstrating his skill but close enough that they could still hear the music that Jim loved so dearly. Scotland was his home in so much as it was where he was born and grew up—and he still had a great deal of patriotism towards it—but for various reasons, it still didn't have the pull to keep him there. He knew this would probably be the last time he'd visit it for many years to come, so he was determined to dwell on its good points instead of all the painful memories that had caused him to leave in the first place.

"Ahhh, it's good to be home!" he said. Maria knew him well enough though to know he didn't mean it too strongly, and there was no danger of him changing his mind concerning their future plans.

As they breathed in the clean mountain air and made observations at just how incredibly beautiful their surroundings were, they gave thanks to God for His creation and for giving them the opportunity to enjoy it. On a different mountain to the one that Isaac and Ricardo were busy conquering, they noticed an injured body being winched to safety by a helicopter, reminding them to pray for the boys' immediate wellbeing as well as that of the unfortunate climber. It was the first time Maria had let Isaac embark on such a dangerous adventure with only Ricardo for company, so she was naturally feeling nervous.

Thankfully the boys returned safely, having made it to within a couple of hundred feet of the top and obtaining some fantastic photographs. Then they all continued north until they reached their destination at a town called Fort William and located their guesthouse. After dinner Jim wanted to show them Scotland's highest peak, which was another short drive away, but by the time they reached it, their enthusiasm for mountains had waned and was replaced by their desire to sleep. And so, as they slept in the car, Maria and Jim took another one of their limited opportunities to spend some time together walking amid the trees at the foot of a mountain until the rain came down in force again.

Back in the guesthouse, the desire for sleep overtook Jim, and he was forced to retire early to his shared room with Isaac. With all the driving he'd done the previous two days, it was impossible to stay awake. It pained him greatly that he was unable to spend some more time talking, just the two of them, and find out Isaac's thoughts on his mom's upcoming marriage, but no matter how hard he tried to fight it, he just could not help falling asleep.

In the morning, after a haggis breakfast, it was back to driving again. Their journey took them across country to Edinburgh, where they spent a few hours taking in the sights and buying more gifts. Then they continued another couple of hours down the east coast into England to where Darius lived; there they met him and Boaby in the bar that Jim used to habitually frequent and still had many acquaintances, many of whom had come out specially to meet him.

Being in bars and around liquor was not Jim's number-one location of choice, but it was also not one of which he was afraid. After giving up the alcohol, he found he was still able to converse and have fun just as much as he was before, but it also let him see in others what was undisclosed to him for so many years—that the objective to get wasted was not such a good one after all. Being back among those who used to share in his experiences, and who were still creating their own, left him all the more grateful when he turned to see his reward for giving it all up sitting next to him, smiling.

"She's wonderful!" said Katherine, the barmaid. "It's so good to finally see you with your life together!"

"Yeah, I thought at one point I'd never be alive to see this day," Jim replied.

"Neither did we," she said, patting him on the back of the head. "Neither did we!"

After saying farewell to the bar, and to Darius and Boaby, they embarked on the rest of the journey back to Jim's house. As Ricardo and Isaac lay sleeping in the back, Jim and Maria listened to music. He put on a CD that one of the talented singers in Maria's church had made, and on which she'd sung backup with her choir, and listened in awe of her as she sang her parts along with the melody. Not only was she beautiful, but her voice was beautiful, and it was nice to be reminded of it.

Unfortunately the final full day of the vacation had to arrive, and to both Jim and Maria, it had arrived too fast. It was their final day before they parted yet again, their final day before the stresses of organizing a wedding and the pains of immigration would no doubt increase considerably, and their final chance to have some fun for what seemed would be a very long time to come.

Jim began the day by checking the computer to see if there had been any change in the status of the immigration petition but was met with the same response he'd had the previous six months and ten days: not yet!

The rest of the day was spent touring London with Ruth, Martin, Stacey, and Samantha. At night they met up with Ruth's friends, Howie and Joan, to take in a West End theatre performance of *The Lion King*. While the rest of the group watched the show, transfixed by its enthralling special effects and enchanting storyline, Jim spent the entire evening with his eyes half-open and his head rocking back and forth, the extensive driving of the last three days having finally caught up with him.

Back in the house everyone retired to their rooms, leaving Maria and Jim alone in the living room.

For some strange reason, Jim felt a compelling force urging him to check the computer again concerning his immigration. Inwardly answering the voice in his head he groaned, *Oh come on! I checked it this morning, just like I checked it every other morning for the last goodness-knows how long!*

Just check it again, came the reply

"Okaayy!" he said, this time audibly, leaving Maria wondering what was going on.

He went upstairs and typed in the same information he'd entered so many times in the past. This time however, he got a different response…

> Your petition has been approved. We have sent it to the Visa Processing Unit (VPU) for further processing, which should take two to four weeks. They will then send the approved petition to the US Embassy in London who will write to you again advising you of the further action required. This approval does not in itself guarantee immigration acceptance, nor may it be used as a visa.

He went charging downstairs to tell Maria then back upstairs again to wake up Ruth and let her know too. With the same kind of glee as someone who'd just found out they'd won the lottery, he embraced Maria as tight as he could and attempted to dance her around in a circle. As he let go and looked at her smiling face, his eyes began to fill with water as the enormity of the situation hit him from all angles.

This was it, the last approval they needed for their marriage to take place in theory. Most people only had the usual people to ask (both sets of parents, families, ministers, etc.), but in their case, they had an added authority to appeal to. Now on receiving the IA's approval, it almost made them want to send a thank-you note in reply.

He could now marry the love of his life, this stunning, gorgeous, beautiful woman who stood before him looking lovingly at him in return, this faith-filled companion who complimented him in so many ways, this blessing from above!

Right behind those thoughts came the relocation implications. Up until that point, it had just been an exercise in paperwork. Now it was real; he would be leaving behind the country he'd just spent the last week touring to take up residence in one far bigger and a lot farther away.

Thirdly came overwhelming thanks to God. The very fact that the petition had been approved without the need for further information or questioning was in direct response to the prayer they had made back in December when they filled out the forms and submitted the documents.

Then, lastly, another dose of reality came along. The petition had been processed in the length of time the initial guidelines had said it would be—between six to eight months. It followed that if the rest of the case were dealt with in a likewise manner, it would still mean it concluding anywhere up to eight more months from now, assuming there were no complications. He felt obliged to remind Maria of this fact, too, as his excitement faded slightly.

"Don't worry," she told him. "It'll all be okay!"

"I know, but–"

"'But' nothing. It'll all be okay!" she said softly. Then, placing her arms on his shoulders and her hands around the back of his head, she gently kissed him before repeating, "It'll all be okay!"

Chapter Seventeen

"Goodbye, my love. This will be the last time we have to do this," said Maria prophetically, trying to hold back her tears at the airport.

"Aye!" Jim said in half-hearted agreement.

"I'll see you in September. I love you!"

"I love you, too ...*so much*!"

She turned to catch up with the two boys who were near the door to the security search area. Jim watched as she showed her passport and tickets to the officer in charge before disappearing from sight, then he trudged slowly back to his car. The journey back to the house was the loneliest he'd ever made, the emptiness felt like grief. Every landmark he passed had Maria's comments about it still echoing in his mind.

Maria managed to compose herself a little longer, even until she made it onto the plane. It wasn't until the monitor showed the flight crossing over Glasgow that the vivid memories of her time there caused the tears to start flowing.

Back in San Antonio, she was picked up by Carmen who—like so many others would—wanted to hear every last detail of her trip. It wasn't long before her tiredness turned into energy again as she excitedly recounted as much of it as she could in the short ride home. It was the same on the telephone the rest of the evening as first her mother and then Jacqueline got to hear all her stories all over again. Alice asked her to pass on her thanks to Jim for treating her daughter "like a princess," and she smiled as she considered how accurate her statement was.

The next days and weeks, it was business as usual as her vacation faded further and further away into the realms of history. If she weren't working, she was sorting things out for the wedding, and if she weren't sorting things out for the wedding, she was working! At least, that was how it felt. And the continuing difficulties at work over staff shortages and heavy workloads didn't make things any easier. Even obtaining three hours off to attend Ricardo's university graduation was a struggle.

In spite of everything, she was still able to make good progress with the wedding preparations. The catering, floral, music, and video arrangements were largely taken care of, and she succeeded in finalizing the outfit requirements of the bridesmaids, the groomsmen, and the flower-girl. She even managed to find a cake-topper of a groom in full Scottish Highland attire standing beside a bride, which her wedding cake designer was able to incorporate into her creation. And in a joint-effort with Jim, the invitations were finally ordered. In a separate exercise, she was thrilled when she added up the projected total cost of their expenditure and found it to be equivalent to the amount they had already saved.

A further boost came when word was received from the Visa Processing Unit, just nine days after the IA approved their initial petition, advising that their case had already been sent to the US Embassy in London. The expected length of time for this to take place had been stated at two to four weeks, so nine days was extremely encouraging and brought with it a heightened sense of optimism in them both.

Jim took more steps forward towards his move to America. Acting on what he could only self-describe as "absurd" faith, he set a date of September 18 as the day his move would take place—exactly one month before the wedding—which would give him time to get used to his surroundings and help Maria with the preparations. In his subsequent resignation from his job, he arranged for his last day to fall the week before the move, giving him time to also have a leaving party with his colleagues in between.

He called Steve and Diane in San Antonio to let them know the news of his arrival date and made sure it was still okay to stay with them until he was married. It would be four months since he last saw them, and they were already missing him like he was one of their own.

He then began finding buyers for his most valuable items—those that he'd held back from his sale at the market in June—and felt similar anguish as they fetched a whole lot less than he originally paid for them.

He did his best to prepare for the package, which the Embassy would be sending him in connection with the next step of the immigration process, by researching online its requirements and requesting documents from outside sources as far as possible. In another welcomed piece of encouragement, one such document, which he was at first disturbed to learn might take up to forty days to be issued, was received in only ten. "*Thank You Lord!*" he rejoiced, making sure God got the glory for every good thing that came his way.

He liaised with Darius over his options for obtaining through him a discounted airfare to Texas. To begin with, he stopped short of booking the flight, still hoping that a clearer picture might emerge in the intervening period as to the *exact* timing of it all—still hoping that he'd have his miracle by then—but as the weeks passed and no package from the Embassy was received, he was pressured into turning his single ticket into a return. The return date would have to be nine days *after* the wedding in what was to be an intensely-heartbreaking, yet seemingly enforced, lapse into the contingency plans he so desperately wanted to avoid.

In another difficult endeavor, he made one last trip north to see Darius and visit his old neighborhood. He went back to the pub where he'd taken Maria and the boys on their visit and said his final farewells to his old drinking buddies, and even though they now belonged to his past, it was still hard to say goodbye. His sadness was lifted slightly when Katherine remarked on how everyone had seen how happy he was with Maria. In the end he was sent away with their blessing and best wishes for his new life, which made the whole experience worthwhile and made him glad he'd decided to go through with it.

And despite all the constant activity leading up to his proposed move, he was able to finally relinquish his dependency on nicotine as he ceremoniously spat out his last piece of gum.

Above all, both he and Maria sought the Lord with everything they had. They spent time in each of their telephone conversations in prayer to God, and often they would type out more prayers in the e-mails they sent each other. The fasting continued one day per week and was later increased to two the closer to the deadline it got. Both received one-on-one prayer from the elders at their respective churches and dwelt continuously on teaching about faith from Christian television, which was becoming an increasingly common topic.

In the midst of all the activity there were, however, some things that they both could have done without.

Jim succumbed to a bad dose of influenza, which laid him low for over a week, consequently reducing his much-needed income. In another instance an encouraging, faith-filled e-mail he sent Maria mysteriously and completely disappeared from existence shortly after she opened it at the exact time she really needed to hear what it had to say. Questions over the timing of their marriage were starting to intensify, as were those doubting the existence of God in it all. And both Maria and Jim were bothered by bad dreams at night and stress and extreme tiredness during the day.

In Jim's case, since his employment was due to end, the volume of work he was given increased. As such, fatigue was affecting his ability to get things done both inside and outside of work, and in the case of the latter, there was much to be done. On top of it all, he was forced to contend with some of the most contemptible passengers he'd ever had the misfortune to meet in all his years of flying. Were it not for Maria's encouraging words and the fact that he was due to be leaving anyway, there was no doubt he would have simply walked away and never looked back.

With not long to go, and in a bid to cheer himself, Jim decided to phone Granny. Granny was seventy-nine years old but had as much exuberance as someone half her age and was always good at raising his spirits. She was also the most faith-filled individual he knew and was no stranger to praying for miracles and subsequently seeing them happen.

"*Hullo Granny*! *How ye doin*?" he said loudly.

"*Oh, hullo, son*!" she yelled back, joining in the over-the-top greetings. Their Scottish accents would always thicken each time they spoke.

"You ok?" he asked, bringing the volume levels down.

"Aye, I'm all right! I'm always all right!" she said. "How you doin'?"

"Ach, not so good. Still stressed out about this visa thing."

"Still not heard anything?"

"Naw. And it's looking more and more desperate! I don't know what to do. I mean, I've prayed and prayed—*we've* prayed and prayed, I mean, both me and Maria—we've fasted, we've spoke out in faith, we've tithed, we've given, we've been listening to teaching…and then we've prayed some more! It all looked good for a while when the paperwork was sent to London, and I thought it was gonna take off from there, but since then it's all gone quiet again, and we're totally running out of time. They said I'd receive a package from the embassy 'shortly,' but that was a month ago. Even then, I'll still have to fill out more forms, and that's when they said it'll take three months or more before I'm offered a medical and an interview. I've had to book a return ticket for when I go over next month with a date after the wedding as when I'm coming back, and I *really* didn't want to do that, but I had to. On top of that, work's a drain, I'm tired, I'm stressed out, I've still got loads to do, Maria needs me."

After finishing his rant, he light-heartedly summarized it all in one word, "*Help*!"

Granny gave a sympathetic laugh. Then she said something he wasn't expecting. "Okay, here's what I want you to do: I want you to *stop* praying!"

"Eh?"

"Aye, stop praying! Let me do your praying for you. So many times when you're in need, you can pray yourself into a frenzy, praying the same thing over and over again and constantly being on high alert and looking for the answer around every corner. Sometimes God just wants us to '*be still*.' So if you can, try and relax and let me and my friend Gloria intercede for you both. Obviously keep talking to God about it. Just stop battering His eardrums and getting yourself all worked up! How's that sound?"

"Sounds good," Jim said. It did indeed sound like good advice, even though in his ongoing state of agitation he wasn't sure if he could adhere to it.

Granny prayed for him over the phone, and he finished the call with a renewed smile on his face. "Thanks Granny—you're the best!" he told her as he hung up.

Clinging to her advice, Jim tried hard to relax and continue in the hope that God would now intervene with the miracle that would save the whole situation. God listened to Granny more than him, he thought! But when the end of August arrived and he'd still heard nothing, the depression from having to rely on Plan B was crippling him.

"Why don't you just phone them up?" Ruth asked him.

Stacey, Samantha, and she were off to a Christian festival three hours north of where they lived, and Jim was driving them there. His road-rage was worse than usual, prompting her to pose the question.

"Because…it's about one pound and fifty pence per minute! And they'll probably just tell you you'll need to be patient!" he snapped.

"But how long has it been since you heard anything?" Ruth asked.

"Over six weeks." Jim replied.

"And how long did they say again it would take before you heard anything?"

"They didn't. They just said 'shortly.'"

"I would still give them a call; what do you have to lose?"

"About ten pounds by the time you eventually get to talk with someone, no doubt!" Jim said with derision.

"I don't mind paying for it. Call them tomorrow." said Ruth.

"You sure?"

"Aye, go for it!"

The next day he rang the premium phone number listed on the Embassy's website. It did indeed take a while before he was eventually able to speak with someone, but the member of staff he spoke with was more willing to help than he thought. When they located his case however, the news was less than good: "We sent you a letter about two weeks ago. Did you not receive it?"

Chapter Eighteen

A postal strike in the UK at the time had seen many letters go missing or undelivered, but for the letter from the Embassy to be one of them was just the *last* thing Jim needed! *Of all the ones for it to happen to, why oh why did it have to be that one?* Jim complained to God.

Fortunately he was given details of what it said over the phone. There was a website link to go onto, and the forms, which in the past were mailed to the petitioner, were now available for download upon the entry of specific information, given to him in the call. Immediately after the call, he phoned Maria to tell her what had happened.

"You're not going to believe this," he started. "The letter we've been waiting for got lost in the mail! The good news though—if you can call it that—is the forms I need to complete can be downloaded from the Internet, so I can get started on them ASAP."

"Oh," was the only thing Maria could say, the magnitude of what he'd just said catching her off guard.

"Aye, so that's that. Unfortunately I've got a wedding reception to go to in a couple of hours time tonight—which I promised I'd attend—and tomorrow I've got a twelve-hour shift to do after church, so I won't be able to start on the forms until Monday, and that's another two days gone. It's not looking good is it?"

"No, it's not, but that's not to say we still won't get the visa in time. We serve a miracle-working God!"

"I know, but..."

"No, 'but' nothing! You know I once heard it said that God likes to stack up the odds against a situation by allowing so many adverse things to happen and then when He *does* come through on time, He gets all the more glory. Maybe that's what He's doing here; we've just gotta keep believing."

"Yeah, I guess," Jim said.

"Whatever happens, we're still gonna get married, and even if we have to wait a bit longer until we're together, I just know it's gonna be worth it."

When they finished speaking, Jim had a look on the Internet at the forms he needed to download and printed them off. Along with the forms came instructions, part of which read,

> During such time as we are in receipt of your information, please do not phone us with case-specific questions as they will not be answered.
>
> Details of the length of time it will take to process your case are as laid down under the "time limits" page of this section. Please do not call or write to us asking for your case to be dealt with sooner than what these limits state as your request will not be heard.
>
> Your initial petition approval in no way guarantees you will qualify for a visa, nor does the submission of these forms guarantee you will be granted an interview. Therefore you should refrain from making definite provisions such as resigning from your job, selling your property, making travel plans, or finalizing wedding arrangements.

Recalling the actions of King Hezekiah in the Bible, Jim approached God in a similar manner (Isaiah 37:14–20). He spread the forms out over his bed, got down on his knees, and prayed, "Oh, Heavenly

Father, You state in Your Word that 'nothing is impossible' to those who put their trust in You. I present to You our case, the forms I need to fill out, and the information I need to obtain and the instructions that say there will be no deviation from the time limits stated. As You can see, these limits state that our case will not be dealt with in the time we have available, yet we believe that You promised us we would be married on October seventeenth, the date You gave us back in December. Oh, Lord, Your word also says that 'faith without works is dead,' and we have done all we know how to—and we will continue to do so—alongside our faith in Your ability to do that which we cannot. I beg You, please work a miracle on our behalf that Your name may be glorified in all of this once it is over, as people hear of our story and recognize that none of it could have happened without Your intervention and praise You for Your miracle-working power. In Jesus's mighty name I pray. Amen and amen!"

In spite of his eagerness to begin work on the forms, Jim remained true to his commitment to attend his friend's wedding reception that evening. It succeeded in taking his mind off things as he watched how happy the couple appeared, bringing on thoughts of how his own wedding would look in seven weeks' time. The groom—an ex-soldier—had bloodshot eyes from all the tears of joy he'd been shedding throughout the day, and it gave Jim comfort in so much as if it were okay for a tough guy like him to cry, then it would be okay for him too! The bride, albeit happy, still had a look of stress about her, which he prayed would not be so with Maria. He also unwittingly found himself *evaluating* their wedding before sadly realizing that people would no doubt be doing the same with theirs.

At home he had another look through the forms and saw that they also required supporting documentation to be presented on the day of his subsequent interview; one such piece he was not in possession of. Since Ruth and Stacey were away, he decided to phone

Darius, primarily just to have someone to talk to but to also let him know what was going on. Darius reminded him that the upcoming Monday was a public holiday in the UK and the missing piece of information would have to wait until Tuesday before he'd be able to request it.

The immigration forms took ten hours to complete that Monday, and he was pleased he had the whole day to complete them. Public holidays were not honored by the airline industry, but by chance Jim had it off anyway. In a bid to break the monotony, he phoned Steve in San Antonio and brought him up to speed with all that was going on. Steve, like Maria, was comparatively calm in his reaction to the report of the setbacks and the seemingly impossible circumstances they found themselves in, choosing instead to pray for him over the phone that God would *definitely* provide the visa ahead of the wedding. It was the most powerful and most specific prayer Jim could ever recall hearing, and he had to draw on the last of his faith reserves to echo his amen at the end of it.

Steve also said he'd ask his Bible study group to step up their prayers too. Meanwhile Jim went back to filling out the forms.

Towards the end he came across one that asked for specific dates of wedding plans, travel arrangements, and medical examination, if already obtained. Such requests seemed contrary to the instructions already given to refrain from such actions; but in keeping with the honesty of the previous information he'd supplied, he felt obliged to record the details.

That's strange! he thought, and then his brain went a step further, *I wonder if it's therefore possible to arrange the medical ahead of time?*

Under the premise of at worst, they can only say no, he located the number of the specialist physician who performed all medicals for the Embassy and called their office the next day.

"Hullo! I'd like to know if it's possible to book a medical for my immigration to America please?" he asked.

"Do you have a case number, please?" came the reply. He proceeded to give them his number.

"And when would you like it for?"

"This week!" he said, boldly, adopting the same principle that they could only either politely decline or laugh in his face! To his astonishment, however, the response was neither.

"It just so happens we can offer you Thursday afternoon. Would you be able to make that?"

"Sure," he replied, trying to remain calm at the amazing news he'd just received. Considering the number of people he imagined wanting to emigrate to the States, he felt sure the waiting list for a medical would have been extensive to say the least. Whether there had been a cancellation or his thoughts were unfounded, right now he didn't care—a huge and important step forward had just been made. And he also had that Thursday off work too!

He returned to the missing piece of information and made a call to the relevant authority in order to obtain it. Their offices were only seven miles away, and in another piece of much-needed favor, he was allowed to come by and pick it up instead of having to wait for it to be sent by mail.

Back in the house, he was now able to finish the forms and sign-off that he was ready to be interviewed. He drafted a covering letter, praying over it both before and after he wrote it, and placed it with the rest of the paperwork. Next he went to the library and made use of their photocopier to obtain duplicates of all he'd done before lastly heading to the post office, where he was finally able to mail everything to the Embassy. Somewhere in the middle of it all, he found time to send Maria some flowers to her office.

Worn-out and mentally exhausted, his day wasn't finished yet. He still had to drive the three hours to go pick up Ruth and the others from their vacation, load up the caravan, and drive it back again.

Ruth was in high spirits when he arrived, having been highly blessed by her time at the festival, and it was difficult for him not to spoil that mood in his tired state. Just before leaving the campsite, his edginess was made worse when the caravan, which had been incorrectly attached to the car by two of Ruth's friends, fell off onto the road. After he reattached it, it dawned on him how much worse it could have been had it come off on the main road, and soon he began to see the incident for what it was—another impediment yet another demonstration of God's favor by causing it to happen when it did.

After a long, rain-soaked journey home, he detached the caravan from the car and hurt his groin in the process. Inside the house he showed Ruth the letter he'd written to the embassy and let her read it. "That's anointed!" she said, referring to the courtesy it contained. Then she began talking about his upcoming move to America and how much she was going to miss him.

"I've only ever wanted you to be happy," she said, with tears starting to form in her eyes. "And it's obvious you are and that it's what God wants for you both. So that makes me *extremely* happy!"

"Want me to stay here?" Jim asked, trying to cheer her up a bit.

"No, it's okay," she replied solemnly, before realizing he was being facetious. "You know, I was speaking to someone at the festival, and they asked me if I was okay about you moving so far away. I said 'I'd rather he was alive in America than dead and in the ground here!'" she said, his past history with alcohol in mind. "So you go. We'll be okay, I promise you. Don't worry."

"I am happy," Jim said softly, his own tears starting to form. Even though there was no need for him to mention it, he decided to say it anyway just in case there was any miniscule doubt in Ruth's mind over his state-of-mind.

"I know," she said and proceeded to give him a hug.

Two days later it was time for the medical, and Jim was more nervous at the thought of that than the actual visa interview he'd later need to attend at the Embassy. The idea that God had already brought him and Maria this far had somehow escaped his attention, and on the train journey into London, he was dogged by thoughts of failing it.

He allowed himself plenty of time to locate the physician's offices then wander around London for a while in an attempt to relax himself, but the nerves would not subside. His thoughts consistently dragged him back to his past problems with alcohol, and it felt like there were fingers being pointed in his direction and voices repeating over and over, "*Loser!*" He recalled how he was required to prove his sobriety more than once to his employers and even more so in his attempts to get his driving license back. How he hoped he'd not have to go through it all again today.

On arrival at the medical, he was given questionnaires to fill out concerning his current health and past medical history. Just as he feared, there was the question about alcohol use: "Are you currently receiving, or have you received in the past, treatment for alcohol or drug misuse?"

He honestly answered yes and proceeded with the rest of the form. The only other matter of concern was a mild strain of tuberculosis he'd had as a youth, which had been successfully treated but nonetheless needed to be declared. As expected, the physician spent a considerable amount of time establishing the facts about his alcohol abuse, adopting a highly skeptical approach to her line of questioning, and a little while on the matter of his tuberculosis. By the end of it he felt drained as he was forced to delve into his past in order to answer her queries.

Unfortunately it didn't end there. The physician sent him away with a letter for his own doctor requesting corroboration of the information Jim gave and a prognosis of his likelihood to relapse.

Jim was furious but at the same time understanding. The request would mean more delay and hindrance to the visa processing, but he was smart enough to appreciate the reasons behind it. All the way home, he linked this latest episode with the other ones in the past in which his abstinence was called into question and asked God, *When is it ever going to end? Am I gonna be haunted by this forevermore? I know I messed up, and, oh, how I paid for it! But will it ever be laid to rest? Do I have to drag it around with me everywhere I go the rest of my life?*

Getting an appointment with Dr. Allegra, his own doctor, historically was not an easy thing to do, but she had always been good to him and had become well acquainted with the family, especially around the times surrounding the deaths of his father and grandfather, so it was in his best interests that he consulted her and not anyone else. And in yet another moment of outstanding good luck, he was offered a cancellation the very next morning. *Thank You Lord, and sorry about before!* he groveled to God afterwards.

Dr. Allegra was true to form and promised her report to the Embassy physician would accurately reflect what he had said himself and her assessment of his current state. She also said she'd let him know when she had faxed it over. But just when he thought things were looking up, the weekend arrived, and it was not until three days later she was able to send it.

"Three more days lost!" he moaned to Maria on the phone. "It's September seventh now, and in eleven days time, I'll be on the plane. I honestly can't see me getting an interview now."

"It could still happen!" Maria responded, trying to remain upbeat herself.

"No, the immigration doctor still has to finalize her report and send it to the Embassy. Even if she did it tomorrow, they would have to then make the decision to offer me an interview, and, ignoring their three-month processing timescale, they've already stated that the interview takes place one month from the date of their letter."

Jim suddenly realized something: if the Embassy were to write to him offering an interview a month from the date of their letter, then it could take place anywhere up to October seventeenth, or even worse—for when the honeymoon was planned or when his family would still be in San Antonio. If successful at the interview, the visa would be issued within seven days of it; therefore, the interview itself would have to take place before October ninth at the very latest to allow time for the visa to be received ahead of the wedding. In such a scenario, the letter offering the appointment would thus need to be sent to him by September tenth. And since it was September seventh, and Dr Allegra's fax had only just been sent, it thereby allowed the Embassy *three* days in which to send him their letter.

"Impossible!" he muttered after coming off the phone to Maria.

Then he turned his attention to God again: *Lord, whilst my situation may now be impossible, You are still the God of the impossible. If it still be so that I will have my visa before the wedding, can I please just ask one last thing regarding it? The interview—can it somehow take place before October begins because I honestly don't think I would be able to cope with it if it were any closer than that to the wedding. I'm already struggling emotionally, and I also need to be with Maria in the run up to it because it'll be too much for her to deal with on her own if I've got to wait here until the week before, or less. Otherwise, please make it for November or later so we can have our honeymoon and a wee bit more time together before I need to come back. Either way, just not in October. Thanks.*

His groin injury from the caravan had meant having to take two days sick leave, and he took advantage of his restricted movement by writing letters to each company and organization with whom he had dealings advising of his imminent emigration. He also put together two more books containing the e-mails he and Maria had sent each other and sent them off to be published. Then with only two days left at work, he chose to ignore the ongoing pain of his injury and went and entertained his passengers for the last time.

By September tenth, he had received no offer of an interview at the Embassy, and he began to relax, resigned to having to return to the UK again in November.

"God's ways are greater than ours," he told Ruth. "He knows what he's doing. I'll still trust and follow Him."

He began packing his suitcase of what few possessions he had left, and before handing in his airport ID, he made final use of his free parking and the scales at the check-in desks to make sure it wouldn't be heavier than the permitted weight when he took it to America the following week. He then went into the office where he had a brief meeting with his boss concerning the lawsuit the passenger was bringing on the company that would now have to be settled in his absence.

After handing back the ID and his uniforms, he walked past the crowds of people scurrying around the airport looking stressed and thought to himself, *Y'know, I really don't think I'm gonna miss this!*

That evening was his leaving party, and a healthy crowd of twenty-three, mainly flight attendants, showed up at the pizza restaurant at which he'd booked tables. Everyone said how much they were going to miss him and especially his humor. His friend Gerry asked if he could continue his legacy and use his jokes after he'd gone, and Jim gladly gave his consent. Until that point he never knew what it was about the job he felt he would miss, but now with those of his favorite co-workers there to honor him, he realized it was *them*. They were the ones who shared in every bad day and horrible experience and were so highly-skilled at supporting each other through them. They were the ones who convinced him to keep returning to work each day despite the ugliness of the job itself. They had become his friends, yet in all probability, this would be the last time he'd see them. It was a surreal experience, yet he still stopped short of telling them he'd soon have to come back to the UK for a little while to tie up his emigration.

At his final appearance at his church on Sunday, he was called out to the front and prayed over by the elders in front of the whole congregation. It gave him a chance to thank everyone for their support of him, especially for the days in which he'd turned up smelling of alcohol (of which there were many) as well as the chance to explain to them all the remaining technicalities concerning his visa. And in a moving tribute to his mother, he gave Ruth a special mention and spoke briefly on the importance on never giving up on people, using her example with him as evidence. "What a sermon!" said Simon, the assistant pastor, as Jim handed him back the microphone.

Afterwards he received a text from Darius. It read,

"Have a blessing filled week. God is going to perform miracles this week before your very eyes."

Calling him to address it, he asked him what prompted him to say what he had.

"I don't know. It just felt like the right thing to say!" said Darius.

"Do you know something I don't?" Jim asked curiously. He had called the Embassy the day before and had been told his case had been passed on, but that could have meant anything as far as he was concerned. Now, together with Darius's text, it seemed like there might be the tiniest speck of hope somewhere in amongst it all, but he was determined not to let himself get carried away.

"Aye, well, if He's going to do something, He's gonna have to do it before Thursday of this week!" Jim went on crudely, referring indirectly to the fact his flight to the States was on Friday.

"You never know!" Darius warned him, chuckling.

Jim spent the next few days trying to spend as much time with his family as he could, meeting up with his closest friends in between, and packing and repacking his suitcase over and over again. Two days before his departure was Ruth's birthday, and he did his best to make it a memorable one for her since it would no doubt be the last one he'd share with her for a while.

Maria was continuing in her efforts with organizing the wedding in between the long hours spent at work. She had managed to have one night away with her family in the countryside the week before but spent the next few days after it feeling guilty that she hadn't used the time on more productive things. And even though Jim expressed his delight at her going, she still vowed she'd use every single minute available to her from that point onward to attend to the arrangements. Ultimately she was only removed from her frantic pursuits when news of the death of one of Isaac's schoolmates reached her, slowing her down enough to make sure he was okay.

Amid the bleakness of the visa situation, neither of them relaxed in their praying or fasting, which in Maria's case was made all the harder by the physical lack of energy it caused. They reminded each other daily to stay strong in faith, believing that it was still not beyond the realms of possibility in God's eyes that immigration difficulties would be resolved in time. And they sought Him in every outlet they could.

Finally Jim's last day in the UK arrived. He had been awake a good portion of the night imagining how he would react if the mail arrived and he found a letter from the Embassy in amongst it all. In such an event, the longing to see Maria would have to continue, his concerns about not being with her in the run up to the wedding would have to be laid aside, and he'd be left explaining to people in the UK why he was still there. Even so, he'd have more time to finish all the things he still hadn't enough time to deal with, and better still, all the darkness surrounding the future would in one moment be lifted. Above all, he'd never doubt God again.

The morning went as expected with all the busyness of one moving overseas being true to form. The only respite he got from it was in his usual call to Maria around 11:00 a.m., which lasted an hour. Then it was back to work again. If nothing else, it certainly passed the time until the mail came in the early afternoon.

When the mailman eventually arrived, Jim was already standing at the door—where he had been for the best part of an hour waiting to meet him. His heart was racing as took hold of the bundle of letters and before looking through them he waved them before God and prayed, *Lord, if my letter is in here I promise I will give You the glory You deserve…after I've finished doing cartwheels that is! And if it's not here, I promise I will still give You glory because it means You know better than me what is best for us all, and I will trust in Your wisdom. Amen!*

Then he raced through the pile of letters, and there at the bottom was…a letter from his cell phone company confirming the extension to his contract he requested! Thinking he might possibly have missed it, he went back through the mail twice more just to confirm the letter from the Embassy was not there. It wasn't. His racing heart sank.

Trying to put on a brave face for Ruth, he went through to where she was in the kitchen and groaned, "It's not there!" Even harder was remaining true to what he'd told God less than a minute ago about trusting Him.

"Well, God knows best," Ruth said as she gave him a hug.

"I really thought it would come today. I really, *really* did!" Jim began crying. "I had this fairy-tale ending in my head like something out of the movies that had me holding my appointment letter and staying behind a wee while longer so that I'd later be standing at the church with my visa in hand at the wedding."

"I know, but they did say it would take three months or more," said Ruth, reminding him of the practical side of things.

"Aye, I suppose. I just had faith it would happen sooner than that. Maybe I just didn't have enough."

Ruth hugged him, as did Stacey who had come downstairs to see what all the emotion was about.

"Looks like I'll be able to come back from San Antonio with you lot and carry your suitcases after all!" he said to Stacey, who, despite her handicap, still knew how disappointed he was. She smiled briefly then went back to consoling him.

He called Maria to let her know then set about attacking his list of things to do the rest of the day. It was no use, though. His enthusiasm levels had dropped so low that he could not be bothered doing anything and each thing that he actually *did* do was with such little effort that it probably would have been just as effective had he left it alone. Evening came and the things he hadn't managed to finish were now of no concern to him; *after all, I'll be coming back again anyway, so they could wait until then!* he thought.

Before going to bed, he sat down at the computer at night and wrote in his e-mail to Maria:

> Well, it's finally here! My last day in the UK as a single man! Next time I'm set at this computer, I'm gonna be married to the most beautiful woman the world has ever seen or known and probably missing you like crazy! I don't know why it has to be this way, but Almighty God has decreed it, so who am I to argue?

After finishing, he went through to Stacey's room where she was staying up late watching TV as she usually did. He hugged her tightly and whispered, "Goodbye Toots! I'll see you in a month's time in San Antonio!" The flight the next day was very early, and he wouldn't be able to do it then. Ruth would be giving him a ride to the bus stop in the morning, so he'd get the chance to repeat the exercise with her then.

All the way to the airport on the bus and on the plane to Texas, he interrogated God over the subject of faith. *I just don't get it,* he started. *Your Word says that if we have faith as a mustard seed we can say to the mountain 'Be removed and cast into the sea' and it will be done. Isn't that what we did all along? We spoke out in faith the whole time, and yet our 'mountain' didn't move! Why? What did we do wrong?*"

As his frustration started to become irreverent, he cut short his line of questioning and sulked the rest of the way to Houston. At Border Control he was asked to explain the reason for his stay, and he nervously explained he was there to get married. When asked why he didn't have a marriage visa, he had to explain the complexities of the backup plans he and Maria were forced to adopt and confirm that he would in fact be leaving the United States again after the honeymoon until the paperwork was completed. The officer in charge seemed uninterested in his story but believed it all the same and allowed him to proceed. It was an experience he hated every time he came to America and one which he'd thought he'd never have to go through again as a visitor, but now here it was again and adding to his misery.

His misery lifted when Maria met him in San Antonio and took him somewhere they could enjoy each other's company before dropping him off at Steve and Diane's house. She filled him in on how the wedding preparations were progressing then held his hand across the table as he lamented to her his sadness at having to leave her again after it was all over. Stopping briefly for air, he looked at her and noticed she was smiling.

"It's okay," she interrupted him. "You know it's going to work out fine in the end. It's just taking a little bit longer than we thought it would."

"I know, I know. I just wanted everything to be perfect for our big day, that's all," he replied.

"It *will* be! You'll be there, I'll be there, and Jesus will be there. How much more perfect could it be?"

"I guess so!"

"We'll be fine. We just need to keep praying, that's all."

"I don't think God wants to hear from me for a while—He probably heard enough of me complaining on the trip over! I forgot to 'be still' like Granny told me to!"

"I'm sure He can handle it!" Maria said softly.

Back at the house, Steve met Jim with his usual gusto and his now-obligatory greeting, "Hey Bro, welcome home!"

"Thank you! Not quite home yet though!" said Jim, trying to put a brave face to his statement. There was no doubt from his reaction he was still left reeling from the rollercoaster ride of emotions he'd been through over the last weeks and months.

"You will be soon though! It's not over yet!" said Steve, optimistically.

"Nah ..." Jim replied, before reminding him of the practicalities and the time limits.

He spent a little more time talking with his hosts after Maria had left them to go to her own house. This time, his tiredness was exacerbated by the upheaval and constant running around that had preceded his journey, and he fell asleep easily when he climbed into bed.

In the morning he was wakened at 7:42 a.m. by a text message coming through on his phone. It was from Ruth; and it read, "Can I call you at Steve's now? Important! X"

Chapter Nineteen

With his eyes still half-shut, Jim called his mother.

"You'll need to come back!" Ruth exclaimed on answering.

"Why, what's happened?" Jim asked.

"There's a letter here for you. I wouldn't have opened it, but I noticed it was stamped by the Embassy, so I thought I should. You've got an interview!"

"When for?" Suddenly he felt more awake.

"For Wednesday, September thirtieth!"

Jim almost fainted at hearing the news. His heart began pounding, and his mind immediately went in all different directions as he contemplated what to do first.

"What are you going to do?" asked Ruth, speeding him along.

"Uh, I suppose I'll need to get hold of Darius and get him to change my flights. I've still got ten days before the interview, so I'll probably stay here another week, though."

"Okay, but remember to give yourself plenty of time to get back in case there's a problem with the flight and to get over the jetlag too."

"Aye, no bother! Who else have you told by the way?"

"Everybody!" she replied, sheepishly, admitting she'd probably informed all those he would've liked to have told himself and stolen his moment of glory.

Not that it mattered to Jim. As soon as she'd said, "September thirtieth," he knew the glory did not belong to him; it belonged to the Lord. Not only had He come through with an interview ahead of the wedding, He had kept it from being in October, just like he had asked. As Jim came off the phone, he slumped face first into his pillow and wept. Turning over onto his back, he looked at the ceiling and spoke aloud, "Thank You! Thank You! Thank You! Thank You! Thank You!"

He began wondering why God had allowed him to travel all the way to Texas before the letter arrived. *Why couldn't it have come on Thursday, just out of curiosity?* he asked Him politely, thinking it might have been punishment for his earlier doubt or perhaps insolence in his prayers. Then as clear as could be, he heard God reply, "You were missing Maria too much, were you not?"

"Oh wow, You're awesome!" he told God.

He grabbed the phone again and called Maria who was already up and about. "I've got some bad news," he said, pretending to be sad.

"What?" she asked.

"I've gotta go back," he started off solemnly before raising his tone. "*I've got an interview*!" he screamed.

Silence.

"Are you still there?" asked Jim.

"Yeah, I'm still here. I'm still trying to get over what you've just said though! When is it?" she inquired, trying to establish the facts before she let her bubbling excitement loose.

"September thirtieth! How cool is that? It means that if I pass it, then I should have the visa by October seventh at the latest, and I'll be able to come over on the eighth and still have just over a week to help with the wedding."

"*Praise the Lord*!" she said. "So when are you leaving to go back?"

"I haven't figured that out yet. I need to get hold of Darius to see what he can do with my flights. I'll probably make it for about the twenty-sixth or twenty-seventh so that I've got time to get over the jetlag before the interview."

"Wonderful! Let me know how you get on with Darius won't you. That is such good news! I'm speechless!"

When they'd finished speaking, Maria began rejoicing and calling her friends who were aware of their situation to tell of the miracle God had done. "God is good!" she pronounced at every opportunity she could. She couldn't wait to be with Jim to revel in the moment together, and after a short while she hastily sped off to pick him up.

Jim sprinted through to the kitchen to relay the extraordinary news of his interview to Steve and Diane, who were overjoyed for him and pleased to share in his delight. Steve immediately gave thanks to God for his answer to prayer and for providing Jim with the visa.

"I haven't got the visa yet," Jim said after he'd finished praying.

"No, but you will!" Steve said with confidence.

Breakfast was almost ready, but there was still enough time to type an e-mail to Darius about his flights. Ruth had already told him the news, so with the head-start, he was quick to respond. He amended the return flight from October twenty-sixth to September twenty-seventh, and with it being on his staff quota, it didn't cost anything to change it. *The blessings are already starting to pile up!* Jim thought.

When Maria arrived shortly afterwards, there was more jubilation and tears of joy, and several times throughout the day, they spent shaking their heads and marveling at the wonder of it all. The fact the visa was still to be obtained had not escaped Maria's notice either, but like Steve, she chose to believe it was now only a formality. Problems arose when Jim let his mind drift forward to the interview itself and in an instant became nervous, worrying how he would conduct himself and what he might say. But with Maria continually re-emphasizing her belief in him, it wasn't long before his faith was back in line with hers. "It would be easier to forget about it and just enjoy the week than to spend it in fear," she said. "It should be even easier now to trust God!"

The week passed by quickly, and Jim got to witness for himself the craziness that was Maria's life at that point in time. He spent most of his days either with Steve or with Jacqueline and her kids and his nights with Maria attending appointments and flitting from one location to the other in adherence to the wedding to-do list. Things that were planned were later superseded, and things not previously considered would suddenly appear. *No wonder she's tired!* he said to himself after only a few days of it all.

At the church both Sundays, Jim let rip with his praise to the Lord like there was nobody else watching, and his tears of worship were blinding his eyes. Maria's smile was wider than ever, and comments on her obvious happiness were numerous. Any opportunity there was to tell of how God had turned their impossible situation around was swiftly met with fervor, and no matter how many times the story was told, it never lost its power.

Soon it was time for Jim to leave, and Maria drove him to the airport. In a scene reminiscent of their parting in London, Maria said, "Goodbye, my love; this will *definitely* be the last time we ever have to do this!"

"Aye. I'll be back soon, I promise," said Jim.

The short length of time between his departure and expected return would not make this separation any easier than it had been in the past. Any length of time spent apart was *too* long! And with such a momentous event as the interview taking place in between, the need to be close to one another now felt even greater.

"You can do it!" Maria called after him as she watched him trudge toward the front of the line at security. He smiled and thumbed his agreement, then turned to make his way to the departure lounge.

The journey back was a good one, and he even managed to transfer onto a much earlier flight from Houston to London, which he viewed as yet another blessing from God. Arriving home earlier than planned, he found an e-mail from Maria waiting for him, which was filled with more encouragement for the task ahead. Ruth and Stacey marked his return by treating to him to a meal at his favorite Indian restaurant. Everything was going great until he checked his pile of papers to make sure they were still in the cupboard in the same way he had left them before he went to America. To his dismay he found there was something missing.

"Did you touch these papers?" he demanded of Ruth.

"What papers?"

"The ones in the cupboard with all the immigration stuff I need to take to the Embassy on Wednesday?"

"No. Definitely not. I've not been in your cupboard at all."

Turning his attention to Stacey he snapped, "Have you?"

"No," Stacey replied truthfully.

"Well, there's definitely something missing!"

"That's spooky!" Ruth said light-heartedly, trying to lift the mood while staying concerned enough to appreciate the severity of the situation. Fortunately the missing piece could be replaced the next morning by another trip to the offices seven miles away where he'd been before, but that was not the issue. Nor was it the sixty pounds it would cost to obtain it. The fact of the matter was that the document in question had mysteriously disappeared from existence, and there was absolutely no accounting for it.

Jim's mind immediately jumped back to his experiences the year before and the preacher he heard in San Antonio when he was worried sick of Maria's feelings for him. The words were still so clear: "Whenever the Devil comes at you with venom and great oppression like never before, you know that you are closer than ever to a huge breakthrough in your life!"

Now, here he was on the brink of the most historic day of his life, and the opposition had become supernatural. He called everyone he knew who would believe him and asked them to pray, and Ruth did the same with her friends when he'd finished.

Meanwhile in Texas, Maria was experiencing setbacks of her own. Isaac developed a serious ear infection, and she was forced to take valuable time off work to attend to him. The "oppression" was certainly being felt by both of them, but Jim chose to look at it as if it was in their favor. "If the Devil had nothing to worry about, he wouldn't be giving us this grief!" he wrote to Maria.

He began thanking God in advance for the visa he now felt certain would be granted him. *After all, if it was likely he was going to fail, there would be no need for the fight back,* he reasoned.

"Praise the Lord!" Maria said when he later told her over the phone.

The following day he went and got another copy of the document he needed to complete his package for the Embassy then he and Ruth headed to London where she'd booked a hotel for the night to save the hassle of traveling early in the morning.

The two spent a lovely evening together, enjoying a meal at a Moroccan restaurant and reflecting on his whole life's journey in bringing him to where he was now. There were tears of laughter and tears of pain, but now as he sat on the eve of the biggest change in his life to date, there were no longer any tears of regret. This was what he'd been waiting for all his life: the chance to prove to himself that he was not the failure he'd spent so many years in the dark convincing himself he was. The chance to prove he could now handle the pressure without first diving for a bottle of Scotch for courage. And, as he saw it, the chance to prove he was now ready to be a husband.

Chapter Twenty

Unable to make use of the hotel's Internet facilities to send Maria a message, Jim chose to retire early. To his surprise he was able to enjoy a pleasant night's sleep and awoke in the morning feeling good. The first thing he did was check his e-mails by way of the Internet facility on his cell phone and was pleased to see Maria had still sent him one. As usual it was full of blessings and encouragement and spoke of her excitement for the day ahead, comparing her exhilaration with the day he first told her he loved her and the one in which he asked her to marry him. There was no doubt in Jim's mind he felt the same. Then, in a stirring finale she sent him on his way with a rousing cheer, "Go get 'em, Tiger!"

More text messages from Darius, Gordon, and Suzie and others from his church followed. It felt good to know so many people were thinking of him. He felt good overall, and despite his apprehension over the task at hand, he was still able to tuck away a large cooked breakfast. Afterwards he and Ruth returned to the room to collect their belongings and pray together.

"Lord, I know You are with Jim," Ruth spoke to God. "Give him Your peace today and also give him the right words to say at each step of the way. We know his marriage to Maria is Your will; therefore, he has nothing to fear but keep him humble enough to be open to Your guidance so that the glory of today will be because of You and not of his efforts alone. In Jesus's name we pray. Amen."

"Lord…help!" Jim added with a smile. Ruth's prayer had already said all that needed to be said.

Walking round the corner of the street in which the Embassy stood, Jim suddenly had a thought that the photographs he had of himself might not be of the standard required. The last thing he wanted was to be asked to return at a later date for failing to follow the guidelines to the exact specifications. He checked his watch—there was still half an hour to go before his appointment—and calmly mentioned his problem to Ruth.

"What? You're kidding! Couldn't you have thought of it yesterday?" she asked.

"No, and I don't know why I thought of it now either!" he replied.

In truth he did have an idea of where the thought came from. They'd prayed in the hotel room for God's "guidance" and were now already starting to see the initial manifestation of it.

Just as God had prompted him to consider his photographs, He also reminded him of a second floor photographer a few blocks away who specialized in photographs for the various Embassies there were in the area. *Please let it be open!* thought Jim, and to his great relief when he got there, it was. The patron said he was used to people with last-minute needs, so he opened at 7:30 a.m., and on checking Jim's existing photographs, he confirmed they were indeed the wrong kind. Posing for new ones he said, "Thank You, Lord!" instead of, "Cheese!"

Arriving back at the Embassy with five minutes to spare, he hugged his mother and let her pray one last quick prayer over him. Since no metal or electronic items were allowed inside the building, he handed his phone and keys to her and arranged to meet up again in two hours. Without his phone he'd be unable to receive any more encouragement or give progress reports to the outside world. Once inside he'd be very much on his own.

He turned to face his challenge and walked slowly toward the gates. It was an imposing building, square in shape, and surrounded by a high iron fence with a security checkpoint in the middle of it. He stood behind a line until he was called and asked to present his appointment letter and ID to an Embassy Official standing by a table outside on the street. When both had been approved, he was ushered to another officer waiting in front of the security checkpoint and was made to repeat the exercise. Finally he was shown inside the booth where his documents were reviewed a third time before he and his belongings passed through the screening equipment.

After clearing the procedures, he found himself inside the building perimeter. He glanced up and saw Ruth still standing on the street corner watching him through the iron fence. There were tears in her eyes, and as he acknowledged her with a smile, he could see her lips saying, "I love you!" He knew she'd be praying for him the whole time he was in there, but still he wished she were allowed inside to give physical support as well. Looking back at the building, he took a deep breath and climbed the stairs. It was now just him and God.

At the front desk, he was again made to show his ID and appointment letter then directed to the large room in which he'd be spending the rest of the morning. He was given a ticket with a number on it: P68

As he walked in, he saw around a hundred people already there. Some were watching the monitors and listening for their number to be called. Others were making final checks through their folders of papers. Most were looking extremely nervous, and rightly so. The Embassy had the power to change peoples' lives forever, either for the good or for the bad, based solely on one decision by one of its officials. It would be either approved or declined. It was a concept not lost on anyone there judging by the look on their faces as they sat awaiting their fate.

He took a seat and stared around some more. On one wall was the flag of the United States; on the opposite was the crest of the Embassy. Above the seats were the monitors listing the numbers already called and in progress, which would change periodically to show the next one. There were P numbers and T numbers, and right then it showed "P58," so he knew he was in for a long wait. Beside them were other monitors giving regulations and instructions on Embassy procedures that would prove to be his reading material for the duration in the absence of a newspaper, which was also not permitted. There was also a refreshments table, but since he had no money with him, he did his best to ignore it.

To his right were the segregated windows at which his affairs would be conducted in a style similar to that of a bank or a post office. As he looked at the officials behind the windows and the serious expressions on all of their faces, he soon found himself talking to God in his head: *Lord, if there is anyone nice in among their staff, can I please be seen by them? Please? Just if there is, I mean. There doesn't look like it though!*

"P59."

His prayers were interrupted by an audible voice announcing the next case to be heard and the number flashing for three seconds on the screen. The T numbers were being dealt with fairly quickly, but this was the first movement in the P's since he arrived. About an hour later he realized that P stood for those seeking permanent residence in the States, while T was for those requiring temporary visas only, hence they were moving faster. Now that he had an indication of how long he was going to be sitting there, he chose to relax more until his own number drew nearer.

His view alternating between the flag and the crest and the monitors, he did indeed feel very much alone. It wasn't long before his thoughts drifted onto Maria:. Right now she'd still be sleeping, but, oh, how he wished she could have been sitting next to him! As his fiancée she could have been, too—the rules made allowances for it—were it not for the obvious reasons why she had to remain in America at that time. He imagined himself with his visa in hand and her by his side on their wedding day, and, becoming emotional, he wiped his eyes and sighed loudly, hoping no one had seen the tears that had escaped.

"P65."

He instantly looked again at the monitor and spotted there were two P numbers displayed! The time at the Embassy was a two-step process, and it became clear that other cases in his category were being reviewed simultaneously at their respective stages. It followed, therefore, that those with the earlier numbers had already completed stage one and were being called for their final stage while those numbers closer to his were just getting started. It also meant his case was closer to being called than he realized.

He reached into his bag of documents and pulled out all the ones he'd need first just to make one final check they were all there and in order, although it was a bit late to do anything about it if they weren't. However, in light of the mysterious disappearance of one of them two days ago still fresh in his mind, he wanted to make sure he wouldn't be embarrassed when he reached the window had it happened again.

Passport, birth certificate, criminal record report, photographs, court disclosure...Aye, it's all here!

Placing it all back into his bag, he then withdrew the evidence he had with him that proved his relationship with Maria was genuine. He'd brought photographs of them together from all of his stays in San Antonio and her trip to the UK, photos of him with her family and ones of each of them on their own. All the cards and letters she sent him were also there, together with his copy of the book he made containing their first five months' e-mails and the invoices for the production of the other two, as well as an invitation to their engagement party in July and a spare one to their wedding. Lastly he'd brought the telephone records in which he'd highlighted in a sea of orange the numerous calls to her house and cell phone (unfortunately he had been unable to print off the text messages they'd sent each other, having kept every single one of them, though not intentionally for the purpose of showing to the Embassy).

He decided to pass the time looking through the photographs, of which there were many, and remind himself of the beautiful lady he was doing all this for. As he did so, a young man sitting two seats away from him noticed he had the same ticket category as him and caught sight of the photographs.

"Is that your wife-to-be?" he asked Jim.

"Aye, that's her," Jim cordially responded, unnecessarily pointing to her in the photograph.

"She's very beautiful," he commented.

"Thank you," Jim smiled. "Are you here for the same reason?" he asked, striking up a conversation.

"Yes, this is my fiancée here," he replied, producing a photo for Jim to see.

"Wow!" Jim said, trying to sound enthusiastic enough to match the man's comments of Maria. In reality he barely looked at the photograph for the purpose of evaluating his fiancée but still long enough to notice that the pair looked extremely happy together.

"Thanks!" he replied "I'm Peter, by the way. So how did you two meet?"

Jim formally introduced himself, then unashamedly began his exciting story from the beginning. About ten minutes later he finished.

"Wow! That is some story!" Peter said, having cheerfully remained attentive the whole way through.

"What about you guys?" asked Jim.

"Oh, we met while I was at college over there. I was over doing some work–"

"P66."

He was cut short in mid-sentence by the announcement of his number over the monitor. "Oh, that's me," he said and got to his feet.

"Good luck!" Jim shouted after him, and turning around again he smiled and thanked him.

"You, too!" he said.

In between Peter returning from his initial stage and Jim's number being called came the announcement of "P67," and then his adrenalin started rising. He put his photographs back into his bag and commenced some last-minute prayers to God, but it wasn't long before a dejected-looking Peter returned to sit next to him.

"How did it go?" Jim asked, trying to ignore the obvious pain on Peter's face.

"Not good!" he moaned. "Kim, my fiancée, forgot to sign the 'Affidavit of Support' form, and I might have to come back at a later date with it. I've got to hang around until someone is able to speak to me further."

"So will you still get your interview today then?" Jim quizzed him with concern.

"I don't know. That's what I'm waiting to find out. They said it could take a while though."

"Aw, man, I'm so sorry! When are you getting married anyway?"

"Not until November twentieth, but I was hoping to go over there as soon as possible because she's having to do all the work while I'm stuck here, and I'd really like to be helping her out as much as possible beforehand."

How familiar does that sound? Jim thought to himself.

"What about you guys? When's your wedding planned for?" Peter continued.

"October seventeenth!"

"Wow, I bet you've been sweating a bit! I hope you get on better than me!" he concluded sadly before letting his head drop into his chest. Just then Jim's number was called.

"P68."

Walking gingerly to his assigned window, he looked up at the US flag in front of him then whispered, "Okay, Lord, here we go!"

In almost robot-like fashion, the lady began requesting the individual items he was required to bring, and he correspondingly handed them over. In front of her was his file with all the papers that he and Maria had submitted since day one with a copy of his medical report on top. Stealing a quick glance at it, he noticed a reference to alcoholism and one about tuberculosis with vertical red lines alongside each to highlight them. *Aw no!* he thought, fearing the worst before promptly issuing a stern warning to himself that it could mean anything and not to worry.

"Getting married are you?" the lady asked.

"Oh yeah!" Jim replied humorously. "Can't wait either!"

"There's a lot of people getting married these days!" she said, with the tone of suspicion in her voice that Jim had assumed would arise at some point. He'd heard lots of stories in the past of people attending these kinds of immigration interviews, and no one spoke favorably of the treatment they'd received. Although this was not the person he ultimately had to convince of the genuineness of his upcoming marriage, he was already experiencing a foresight into how he thought it was later going to go.

"Okay, we need you to take this piece of paper to window number nineteen round the corner and pay the processing fee and then come back," the lady ordered him.

Following her instruction, he went and paid the fee then returned to his window where he was asked to sign certain forms, take receipt of the originals of his items she'd copied while he was away together with the chest x-ray he'd had taken at his medical, then sit back down again. He was also given another form to fill out to be handed in again later that requested details of how and where he would like the visa to be sent ("if approved"—as was written as a reminder on the form that he wasn't quite there yet). With everything having been in order, he had just cleared stage one.

He looked for Peter but couldn't see him, so he chose another seat on his own. The P numbers in the sixties of those now in their second phase were at P63, so he knew he would have at least another hour to wait before being called a second time.

After filling in his form, he let his thoughts run wild again. First came the conversations in his head as he tried to think of every question he thought they might ask him and what his answers would subsequently be. Then came a fear of being unable to control his nervousness in front of the interviewing officer, giving them perhaps an impression of dishonesty. To end with came the negative thoughts again—with all the what-ifs in the event of the visa being denied—and the constant need to rebuke them. Once again it was back to feeling alone as he sat shuffling around in his seat. Not having his cell phone and being able to communicate with others was frustrating, too, especially since Ruth would soon be outside expecting him any moment. It was just him, his prayers, and the will to spend the rest of his life with Maria that kept him going.

"P68."

On hearing his number, he took a deep breath and exhaled slowly. Then he rose to his feet, looked to the heavens, and clenched his fist in anticipated triumph as he once again addressed God, *This is it!*

He walked up a short hallway, and on arriving at another window, he found a young man of a similar age to himself reviewing his file. He had a different air about him from the others he'd earlier been watching from his seat, and as he waited for him to acknowledge him standing, there his pounding heart rate strangely began to slow.

"Hi, how are you?" the man asked him.

"Oh, a wee bit nervous but otherwise I'm pretty good!" Jim said with a smile.

"Don't be nervous," he told him. "I'm the nice guy here! If you'd gotten her next door, you'd really have been in trouble!" he joked, referring to his colleague at the adjacent window who pretended not to hear.

Right at that moment, Jim wanted to cry tears of joy as he recalled his earlier prayer to God asking to be interviewed by someone nice if such a person existed. Inside the officer's joke contained the clearest answer to prayer he could ever recall hearing in his whole life, and the subsequent peace that filled him from head to toe could only be attributed to the awesome handiwork of the Holy Spirit!

Oh God, You're so good! he had time to offer up in silence before the next question.

"So…tell me how you both met," the officer asked.

For the second time that day, Jim began rattling off the details of how he'd met Maria after first seeing her on a visit to a church festival in San Antonio two years before. This time he only got as far as his trip a year later before the officer halted him. "That's some story!" he said, laughing. "So when is the wedding?"

"October seventeenth," Jim answered. "I know we're cutting it a bit fine, but we've been believing in faith that all would go ahead as planned."

"Well, we won't hold you back," he said.

"Do you want to see all the stuff I brought?" asked Jim, thinking it was all too good to be true.

"No, that's okay. Your story is the best I've ever heard…I'm sold! I just need to clarify a couple of things about your health, and then you can be on your way."

He brought up the subject of Jim's previous problems with alcohol and was easily satisfied with his word that it was confined to history. Similarly with the issue of the tuberculosis. Then, stamping "Approved" on the top paper, he closed the file over.

"Okay, that's it! All the best for the wedding!"

"Thank you!" Jim beamed. "Do you want to come? I've got a spare invitation here."

"I'd love to! I bet it will be quite an occasion," he said. "I've got to work though," he added, just in case Jim was being serious in his offer.

The whole interview had lasted no more than five minutes. He took hold of his bag and the form he'd been given, and with a huge grin on his face, he headed back into the main waiting area. He noticed Peter had returned and was sitting there, still looking despondent. Thinking it would be improper to walk by without saying anything he stopped to ask how he was getting on, all the while trying to keep his emotions in check a little while longer and not appear too boastful of his own success in the face of Peter's adversity.

"Oh, they're gonna let me come back next week provided Kim can resend the form signed this time. I'm just waiting for them to print me off another appointment letter," Peter said sadly. "It just means another week has to go by before I can be with her, that's all."

"Ah, mate, I'm so sorry again. I hope it all works out for you," Jim sympathized. He fully understood Peter's pain. Had that happened to him, he would've been distraught at the thought of more time away from Maria, so as he left him to his sorrows, he asked God to bless their marriage and make sure everything went well for them from thereon in. Yet as he took his place in line to arrange and pay for the delivery of his visa, Peter's plight soon faded from his memory and was replaced by his own euphoria again.

Standing in line and going over the interview again in his head, he questioned himself, *Did that really just happen?* Then the clerk at the counter called him forward and said, "Congratulations," straight away confirming it to be true. At that moment his life had indeed changed forever.

As he left the building, he began playing out how he would tell his mother. The idea of looking sad and pretending that it was bad news was instantly foregone when he caught sight of her through the fence at the corner where she'd been, praying, for the last hour. Addressing the anxious look on her face, he gestured with his thumb that he'd succeeded and watched as she placed both hands over her face to hold back her tears, which had began flowing. He passed through the security checkpoint again and, once out the door, ran to meet her while she remained standing where she was on the corner, numb. Taking hold of each other, they wept uncontrollably, not caring who was passing by or what people might think.

"Thank You, Lord!" Ruth said, acknowledging God's answer to her prayers. Wiping her eyes and turning back to Jim she asked, "So what happened?"

He told her the details of the interview itself and how the Embassy Official was sold on his story alone without the need for any more evidence. "I'll tell you the rest later," he said, interrupting himself. "I've got a phone call to make first."

Taking repossession of his phone from Ruth, he dialed Maria who had been awake since 4:00 a.m. thinking about him and praying.

"Hello," she said excitedly when she saw it was Jim calling.

"We got it, baby! We got it!"

"Oh Jim!" she sobbed.

"Aye, that's it—it's all over! You can phone Rodrigo now and tell him we're officially getting married! God is *so* good!"

Maria was mainly silent as the details of his account of God's undeniable goodness left her speechless; a few times he had to pause just to make sure she was still there. He imagined her smile and pictured himself hugging her and expressed his regret at not being able to share the moment with her in person. In closing he told her how much he loved her and promised to call again later in the day with the full version of everything that had gone down.

In Maria's case, with her excitement levels now raised to the maximum, it was the first time in a long while she actually looked forward to going to work since she'd have people there with whom to share in her joy. Even though most of her colleagues were ultimately more focused on their own personal miseries, it was still a chance to unburden herself of some of the emotion that was inside her.

Similarly Ruth began phoning everyone she could think of to spread the news, starting with her best friend, Ailsa, in Scotland to allow Jim the privilege of phoning Granny himself. It was difficult for him to hear himself speak over the jubilant shrieks Ruth was making next to him as she rang one person after the other. Eventually he suggested they start walking back to the hotel, where they'd left their overnight bags, in an attempt to regain some degree of normality.

After collecting the luggage, they headed back on the Underground to the station where they'd left the car before journeying back to the house. Jim did the driving, allowing Ruth more time on the phone where it was likely she would've stayed the rest of the afternoon had it not been for a 2:00 p.m. medical appointment with Stacey to break things up. In a brief moment of respite in between calls, he announced proudly concerning his move, "I'm going home, Mammy! I'm *finally* going home!"

"I know," she said, a tear forming in her eye again. "And you'll be safe there, too. Apart from you finding someone who'll love you more than I do, that was the only thing I ever wanted for you—that you would be safe."

Then composing herself, she went back to her phone calls.

At night the family went to the Indian restaurant to mark the occasion, as was their usual practice whenever there was something to celebrate. They were well known by the manager there and always made to feel welcome. However, just like he'd done so often in the past, the manager brought everyone at the table a free liqueur along with the check, and just like every other time, they were obliged to point out they were not ones who liked to consume alcohol. This time, though, Jim laughed at the irony of it. "One last time to try to get me to have a drink, eh?" he said. Then turning to the family he said, "Who needs alcohol when you've got Jesus?"

Back in the house, he called Maria who had purposely taken a later lunch break so that she could spend time talking to him in the middle of the afternoon. They spent almost the whole hour poring over the events of the day and those leading up to it and reminding themselves of what an awesome God they served. Then after the call had finished, Jim went straight upstairs to the computer to send her his regular evening e-mail. He titled it "Goin' Home!" and in it he wrote,

> All my life I've been searching for a place to call "home" and for someone to share it with. I've moved house over fifteen times in my lifetime, each time wondering and hoping that the next move would be the one that would finally allow me to settle down (a bit like Quantum Leap—I love that show!). And so earlier in the car it dawned on me that I finally do have what it is I've always wanted in life—a place to call home! In one single moment when that visa was authorized, all my dreams finally came true!
>
> Of course, technically all my dreams came true when I met you and we fell in love. But there was still that one final piece in the whole puzzle before I could stop dreaming, and that was just a place for us to call home. I'm so happy to now be able to call San Antonio my home; or more importantly, *our* home!
>
> Can I just thank *you* for all your input, support, prayers, encouragement, blessings, advice, wisdom, smiles and—most importantly—love! I could not have ever embarked on such a

> huge undertaking and experienced such a big manifestation of faith had it not been for you being alongside me every step of the way! You've always been my rock, you've never ridiculed me or made me feel small, and you've loved me far beyond anything I could ever have imagined possible. *Thank you*, my love, thank you so, so, so much! I truly do love you more than you'll ever know!

He closed the computer and reached for his Bible. It fell open at the book of Psalms and it read, "For the Lord Most High is awesome! He is a great King over all the earth!" (Psalm 47:2).

He shared it with Maria in a text then went and said his good-nights to Ruth and Stacey before finally slumping heavily onto his bed. Maria sent a text in reply, thanking him for the scripture, which reached him just as the tiredness from his busy day was taking full effect and his eyes were starting to close. He read it, smiled, then fell sound asleep, where he lay in the same position until morning.

Six hours behind in Texas, Maria's day was not yet over. Having been met with little reaction to her news from her colleagues at work, she was determined to share it with people who were spiritually astute enough to recognize the glory of God in it all. That evening she had choir practice, and on arriving, she asked Tim if she might be allowed a minute at the end with the microphone to share her testimony. Even though speaking in public left her feeling awkward, she was determined to give God the credit He deserved. Tim agreed, and when her turn came, she addressed the one hundred and fifty or so in attendance, "Most of you know that I was handpicked by God Himself to take on the relationship of a lifetime. What I wanted to do tonight was give God the glory He deserves for the miracles He's done in our lives. So many miracles have taken place, but the biggest one is how God orchestrated the visa paperwork. From the signing of the application to the granting of the fiancé visa is usually at least fifteen months. We've received the okay to be blessed with the visa in nine months and five days!"

Everybody in the room cheered and started clapping. A huge smile appeared on her face, and her complexion became flushed. Then Tim reminded her that not everyone was aware of her relationship with Jim and made her give a brief summary of it from the start. Just like the time she'd done it before, there were good-humored heckles from some in the group who were determined that she leave nothing out. "It's her story. Let her tell it like she wants to!" Tim interjected, trying to help her out in the midst of all the hilarity.

Shaking all over she finished giving her account and sat down to more applause. There were people patting her on the back, giving her all-round encouragement for her efforts and agreeing with her on God's goodness. As if she didn't already feel special, now she felt it even more!

After the clamor of people wanting to know more of her story eventually subsided, she went home where she read Jim's e-mail. His words were the perfect end to a lovely evening, and she thanked the Lord for blessing her with such a wonderful fiancé and kind friends. Then she began typing her reply, letting Jim know all that had happened to her that day and how unbelievably happy she was. She concluded once more by letting him know how much she loved him and how grateful she was for all his hard work. And in a poignant recognition of the depth of feeling behind the title of his message, she responded in kind,

> Welcome home, Honey. Welcome home!

Chapter Twenty-One

Jim awoke the next morning wearing the same smile as the one with which he'd fallen asleep. With the stress surrounding the visa having now been removed, it was the first time in nine months he was able to look at the future with clarity and walk free of the burdens that had been weighing him down for so long. Despite all the things that still needed to be done ahead of his move, he decided to award himself the day off, choosing rest and relaxation and not allowing anything to get in the way of it.

How Maria wished she could afford herself that same luxury! With just over two weeks to go until the wedding and less time than that at work, it meant she had a seemingly unending list of things to do the whole day long. To add to it all, she now had to drive across town to a bi-weekly practice of a dance performance in which Isaac had been asked to take part. Then came the early morning phone calls with Jim and the e-mails at night cutting into what little time she had left for sleep.

Apart from work, she didn't really mind any of it. She was still on a high after hearing the news of Jim's visa, and the thought of him arriving in only one more week made everything more exciting. Sending e-mails had still not ever become a chore, and Isaac's involvement in any activity was of paramount importance since there was little else she loved more than to see him interact with others. It was all just so tiring.

Jim continued to reward her efforts with encouragement and praise. One more week and he'd be there to help out and there would be no more need for waking at 4.30 a.m. to speak with him or staying up late to write. Yet when it came to the e-mailing, in a strange way she felt a little sad that she'd no longer get to read the words in which he so beautifully expressed his love for her. Sensing he might feel the same, she put forward a notion that they occasionally send each other messages *after* they were married, just to keep alive the memory of how they had arrived at where they were, and to her delight he was pleased to go along with the idea.

Then, in what she viewed as another example of God's favor currently operating in her life, she was rewarded at work with the offer of a new position, one that would involve a much lighter caseload and in turn a lesser strain on her health. But just as how the e-mailing had similarly become an integral part of her life, she wondered how she'd be able to adapt to the pace at work without the heavy pressure she'd become so familiar with to drive her on (in the end she volunteered to help her colleagues in the department she was leaving behind any time her future workload became too light).

Everything was changing, not least of all for Jim who at times allowed the magnitude of this new chapter in his life to cause anxiety. There was no denying it was the biggest undertaking of his life to date, but the prize at the end of it would always far exceed any fears he might have. Each time they arose, he would simply look at Maria's picture, give thanks to God, and remember His overwhelming goodness in providing him with his "masterpiece" (as he called her). She too helped him with some kind words of encouragement of her own, recognizing in advance the challenges he faced, and reiterating her promise to never leave him. *If ever the term "a match made in heaven" were applicable*, thought Jim, *then this is it!*

The favor of God was at work in others' lives too. Stacey received news that she had been approved for an apartment of her own, which with daily supervision would see her gain the independence from Ruth she felt she was now ready to attain. It would mean for the first time in nearly thirty-five years, Ruth would be living on her own, but that was insignificant next to her delight in finally seeing all of her children happy.

Ruth received an answer to prayer herself when Harry, a close friend of the family, made a last minute decision to come to Texas to attend the wedding. He had plenty of experience of driving in America, having previously spent much time in Nevada, so it meant that the group's anticipated transportation problems could now be resolved with the hiring of a minibus once there.

Granny was blessed when results from blood tests she'd recently taken showed no abnormalities in her health, and she was now completely cleared to travel overseas. As was so often the case, she attributed the news of her wellbeing to her abundant trust in God and the fact He was always looking out for her. Even so, she told Jim, it was unlikely she would have missed the wedding if the tests *had* shown up problems—all she had to do was pray!

And Martin was honored when Jim asked if he'd be an usher at the ceremony and individually escort Ruth and Granny down the aisle. He'd previously been declined the best man's position, so to still have a part in proceedings was a special feeling for him.

The only downside, from Jim's point of view, was that Gordon and Suzie were now unable to attend the wedding due to a flare-up of a previous illness that Gordon had, which prevented him from flying. To Jim it felt like the second time he'd been denied a father-figure at his wedding. But he later smiled as he recalled a dream in which he saw his own father giving his approval of Maria and guessed God might allow him special permission to watch the ceremony on his TV in heaven.

On October sixth Jim's passport was returned from the Embassy with his visa inside. As soon as he received it, he got on the phone to Darius to arrange his flight to Texas for the very next day. Then he went to visit Gordon one last time before returning home to spend the rest of the day and evening with Ruth and Stacey. His suitcase was already packed, and the last item on his list of things to do had been taken care of. There was now absolutely nothing to hold him back, except maybe the tears of his family upon realizing the time had now come for him to finally say goodbye to his life with them. He was able to override the sorrow of it all with the concept that it would be just over a week before they would be together again in San Antonio, but he knew there would be a time beyond that when being absent from each other would be a whole lot longer than it would be this time round. It would be even longer before they saw him in the UK again, and neither scenario was without pain.

Before going to sleep, he sent Maria an e-mail for the last time from his computer in the UK. He titled it "The Last One," but all the emotion of the day had drained him of the energy to be able to come up with something inspirational. It ended on a tired-sounding whimper instead of it being the triumphant finale he'd always imagined it would be. But in a last-ditch attempt to redeem himself he concluded:

I LOVE YOU!!!

Switching off the computer, he went into Stacey's room and hugged her. Just like the last time he left for Texas, his flight was early, so he wouldn't be waking her in the morning. As he left her room, he could hear her crying behind him.

After a few hours of sleep, he got up and dressed himself in the same suit he'd worn to the Embassy the week before. Ruth was up and handed him the sandwiches she'd made for him to take to the airport for his breakfast, and she then opened the car for him to place his suitcase and hand baggage inside and took her seat at the wheel. Before joining her, Jim made one final tour of the house, ceremoniously stopping in every room to take mental pictures and playfully waving each one goodbye. He kissed Stacey on the cheek, and without opening her eyes, she smiled but went straight back to sleep again. He took one last look at the computer on which he'd sent Maria so many e-mails and sighed at the idea he'd never have to do it again from so far away. Then back downstairs, he inhaled deeply as he closed the front door behind him and climbed into the car.

At the bus stop, Ruth prayed over him and gave thanks for all God had done in allowing him this new opportunity in life and, more specifically, for giving him such a wonderful lady with whom to spend the rest of his life. She loved Maria and reiterated to Jim how happy she was to welcome her into the family. After she had finished, Jim took hold of her and embraced her tightly, and letting go he said, "I wish Dad could've been here to see this day."

"I know," she said. "I miss him too. He'd be so proud of you!"

The coach pulled into the stop, and Jim stowed his luggage and showed the driver his ticket. He hugged Ruth one last time then got onboard and sat down and looked out at her crying. He could see her say, "I love you!" through the window, and as the bus pulled away, he knew that for the next nineteen hours until he was with

Maria again, he would have to deal with all of his emotions on his own.

Once the town where he lived was behind him, he called up his e-mail account on his cell phone, and there was an message from Maria. It began,

> It's hard to believe that everything that we've prayed for, fought for, claimed as our own, prophesized into existence, stepped out into faith for, is finally here. Our smiles will be big, but not as big as our Father's in heaven! I can just see Him now, smiling at His two special children who looked to Him for the answers, looked to Him for the courage, the strength, the ambition to persevere. We are now being able to reap the benefits for our faith in Him. Nothing we did allowed us to get where we are, apart from being favored and loved and being obedient to Him. If only the whole world knew this feeling; to be a favored child of God!

He nodded in agreement with her summary of things and felt a warm glow as he pictured God smiling down on them, His peace now filling his heart. He reminded himself again of what he was gaining in Maria, this sweet, loving, kind, beautiful, amazing God-fearing woman…It was all his dreams coming true at once. As he made one final study of the familiar landmarks along his journey to the airport, the sadness he thought he'd feel was now notably absent, replaced by his awe of God and the excitement over his future.

The rest of Maria's message was full of her customary buzz and excitement, putting his drab effort the night before to shame. She'd sent him some memorable ones in the past, but here it seemed like she'd saved the best for last. And in what he deemed was probably the finest she'd ever written, she finished off,

> God is fun…just get in (on board) and hang on! For the believer, everyday can be different, but the mission is the same: spread/share the gospel of Christ. God is not boring! We can

choose to see our lives as an adventure, and He is the driver of the boat, car, plane, safari truck, submarine, hot air balloon, jet, bus, ship, train…anything.…He is in charge. If we trust Him, He will let us have the time of our lives, every single day! I'm up for it…!

Chapter Twenty-Two

Sitting on the plane, Jim puffed up his cheeks and blew out slowly as the aircraft took off. He glanced upwards and acknowledged God with a smile. "Thank You!" he whispered.

He had been upgraded to business class. *Not bad for sixty-seven dollars!* he thought, referring to the ridiculously low price he paid for the ticket through Darius. The extra-comfortable seat was now just the latest in a long line of blessings he'd received in recent weeks, and with ten hours to spare before landing in Houston, he took a few moments to count them.

The biggest and most treasured blessing of all was Maria herself. He recalled the first day he met her and laughed as he pictured the blank look on her face the first time he nervously spoke in his thick Scottish accent. He saw the table where they sat for lunch and took himself back to the conversation they had on the phone later that night. Knowing now how difficult the journey had been in bringing them to where they were today, would he still have continued with it had he known back then? Then he answered his own query with a yes! Once he had met her that first time and experienced her character and felt the special bond she had with the Lord, there was no turning back no matter what the cost would be. He would do it all again if he had to!

Next he remembered the initial e-mails, the first time he said, "I love you!" and the joy at hearing her reciprocate, the later anguish of not knowing if she was having second thoughts and then the hug that eradicated it all, the elation at becoming engaged and the first kiss, the subsequent trips to San Antonio and her trip to the UK, and finally the circumstances surrounding the obtaining of the visa. In between he acknowledged the parts played in it all by Steve and Diane, by Darius, Ruth, and Granny. And as he considered each moment, he was able to pinpoint *exactly* where God had been at every time. "God You truly are awesome!" he said softly.

Dwelling for a moment on all the struggles there had been over the immigration procedures, he was reminded of the dream he had when he visited the north of Scotland the previous year. The specific battle he sensed was on the horizon back then had indeed taken place and was now over—the fight there had been to allow his marriage to happen had been won. And just like He said He would, Jesus had been alongside him the whole time.

Ten hours passed slowly, and most of it was spent just contemplating the past. He felt tired and had tried to get some sleep, but his over-active brain would not let him. On arriving in Houston, however, his energy levels were soon restored as he reached the immigration desk and was formally welcomed into the country.

"Welcome to the United States," the officer greeted him. "What is the purpose of your visit?"

"I'm here to stay!" Jim said, with a huge grin on his face. He handed over a sealed envelope he'd been given by the Embassy along with his passport containing the visa.

After the obligatory photographs and fingerprints were taken, he was escorted to a small room for his documents to be verified and final clearance given. Half an hour later, he was released, and after clearing Customs, he walked through the exit-door and onto the next stage of his journey.

He was now officially a resident of the United States of America.

The flight to San Antonio was delayed forty-five minutes due to a security breach within the airport, but it wasn't enough to quell his excitement of his new life that had now begun. When he eventually arrived at his final destination, Maria was waiting with Isaac. Letting his hand-luggage fall to the floor, he grabbed hold of her tightly and hugged her with everything he had while Isaac watched on, wondering if he'd ever let go!

"Welcome to America!" Isaac said.

"Welcome home, baby!" Maria added.

At Steve and Diane's house, he received a similar greeting. They welcomed him into their home to stay one last time and entertained him during the few days Maria had left at work. Just over a week later, he would be living with his new wife, and Diane felt a small degree of sadness at the thought that she and Steve would no longer be the ones he relied upon. "Don't y'all forget to visit!" she warned him playfully. Steve kept up his usual mischief when he said he'd only be able to pick up one of them from their honeymoon and the other would have to walk!

Jim's family and friends arrived the following week, with Darius getting in a day later. The night before the wedding, all seventeen of them met up with around twenty-five from Maria's side for the rehearsal dinner, at which Jim gave a short word of thanks for their attendance before giving even greater thanks to God for authorizing it all. His friend Hamish, who had come over from Scotland, commented to Ruth on how unbelievably happy Jim and Maria looked together and questioned their "secret."

"Jesus ..." Ruth replied, "They've got Jesus."

The next day Jim and Darius got dressed in their Scottish Highland attire and posed for photographs at the house for Diane. Before being driven to the church, Jim took his best friend aside and praised him for his endurance in sticking by him the last twenty-four years especially for those times he wasn't sure he would survive another day. He recognized his patience and kindness and the sacrifices he made and soon the first of many tears that day began to flow as they reflected on where they were now.

At the church Jim sat in the waiting room and continued to ruminate. He'd once told God that if He ever provided him with a wife, then he'd be open to do absolutely *anything* for Him in return. Reminding himself of that promise, he pondered what the future might hold now that God had come through with His side of the bargain.

As he peered out at the crowd of people that was beginning to form, he heard music start up. Maria had obtained a CD of her friend singing at a church performance before he died earlier that year, and his voice was unmistakable. Those who were there who knew the voice began to listen intently, and a few even shed tears, Jim included. He had met her friend and knew how earnest he was in his desire to sing at their wedding. But now, in the way it was meant, his wish had been granted even though he couldn't be there in person.

During the song Martin performed his duties perfectly, escorting first Granny to her seat and then Ruth. Jim then led the procession of males onto the stage to await the arrival of Maria. He was followed by Darius, then Isaac, Steve, and Ricardo. As the organist played, the bridesmaids made their individual entry: first Carmen—Maria's Matron of Honor, then Angeline, Stacey, and another of Maria's close friends, Fay. Then a single bell began to chime…

Making her entry alongside her brother Mannie, Maria walked slowly to the altar. She was smiling, as she had been all morning and afternoon until that point, and like so many times in the past when he saw her smile, Jim's heart began to beat faster. She looked stunning in a way that was far too difficult for him to ever put into words…his knees were starting to buckle, his eyes were filling with tears yet again, and his teeth were clenched tightly as he tried desperately not to let his emotions escape all at once. Had he done so, there was no doubt he would have wept uncontrollably; the ceremony would've had to be delayed until he composed himself, and there was no telling how long that might have taken!

He took Maria's hand and walked her up the stairs to the altar where Rodrigo was waiting "You look amazing..." he whispered to her. "*So* beautiful!"

Before the ceremony commenced, John led the congregation in song to the hymn "Amazing Grace." It had been Jim's choice to sing it, but since he himself had been saved by grace and could fully identify himself with the "wretch" referred to in verse one, he had never been able to get through it without breaking down and crying. Today was no different. Then came the words of the third verse:

> Through many dangers, toils and snares,
>
> I have already come.
>
> T'was grace that brought me safe thus far,
>
> And grace will lead me home.

If ever the words of a song rang true to his own life, they were those. In his case, however, grace had not only brought him through the perils of life in which he'd once placed himself, but now that he was standing next to Maria in the biggest day of his life, grace had also indeed now led him home.

He remembered the advice of Rodrigo from the rehearsal the night before telling him to bend his knees while standing and tried to apply it. It wouldn't stop his tears, but it would at least stop him from keeling over. The fairy-tale ending to the story of his life was unfolding right here and now, and the emotion was almost too great to bear. Only a great deal of inward praying to God to hold him up allowed him to make it through the rest of the wedding unscathed.

The ceremony flowed superbly from start to finish, and neither Jim nor Maria could have wished it had gone any better. Rodrigo pronounced them "husband and wife" and even the kiss to seal their union was perfect.

Walking slowly to soak up the adulation of those in attendance, Jim led Maria back down the aisle and into the waiting limousine she'd been blessed with free-of-charge from a friend. Before getting in he paused to admire his beautiful bride and to tell God once more how grateful he was for his masterpiece. And in a further moment of appreciation, he glanced over at the main road and reflected on the irony of how it had all begun two years before with the taxi he had let go by in favor of the cigarette he wanted to finish.

None of this would have happened had it not been for that one cigarette, eh? he inquired of God, laughing at how his life had changed as a result of that one decision. *To get me to this day and in providing me with my beautiful wife, You even used a cigarette!*